KT-197-617

SECRET
TUSCANY

Carlo Caselli

Jonglez

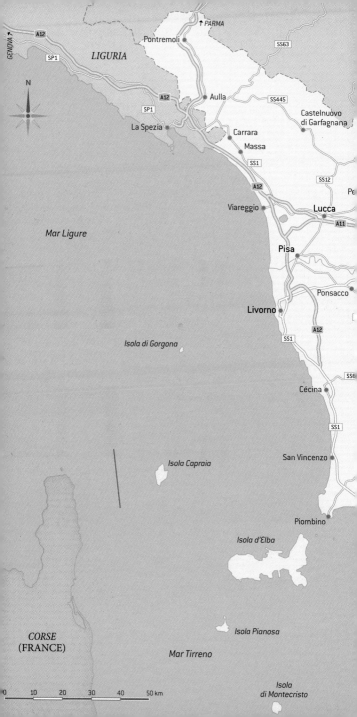

Secret Tuscany is the result of an observation: the guidebooks available to the inhabitants of Tuscany and frequent visitors to the region all seem to describe the same familiar places. There is nothing or very little in them that would surprise anyone who already knows the region fairly well.

This guide is aimed at such readers, although we hope it will also please the occasional visitor seeking to depart from the beaten tourist paths.

Comments about this guidebook and its contents, as well as information concerning places we may not have mentioned herein, are more than welcome. They will permit us to enrich future editions of this guidebook.

Don't hesitate to write us:
• By e-mail: info@jonglezpublishing.com
• By post: Jonglez publishing -
   17, boulevard du Roi 78000 Versailles France

CONTENTS

OUTSIDE FLORENCE

CONTENTS

PISA

LUCCA

CONTENTS

NORTH WEST

LIVORNO AND SURROUNDINGS

GROSSETO AND SURROUNDINGS

CONTENTS

AREZZO AND SURROUNDINGS

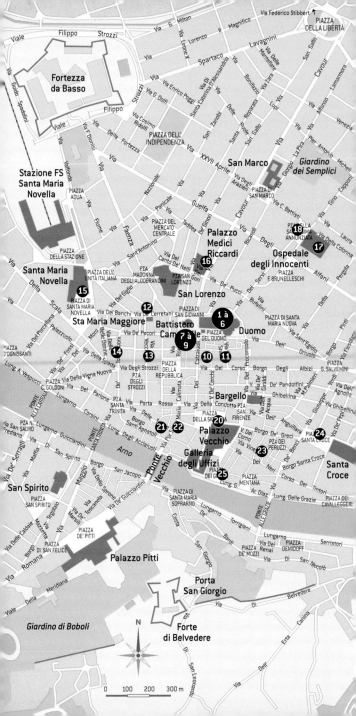

FLORENCE

OBSERVING THE SUN WITHIN THE CATHEDRAL ❶

Piazza del Duomo
• Opening hours of the cathedral: Monday to Wednesday 10.00-17.00, Thursday 10.00-15.30, Saturday 10.00-16.45, Sunday and holidays 13.30-16.45.
• Free admission.
Solar observations, with an explanatory commentary provided by an astronomer: about four times a year, in the month of June. The exact dates are given on the internet site: www.operaduomo.firenze.it. Entrance is by the Porta dei Canonici (southern side of the cathedral). You should point out to the custodians that you want to see "*la meridiana*".

> *An extraordinary astronomical phenomenon*

Around four times a year, roughly coinciding with the summer solstice (June 21), the cathedral of Florence provides an extraordinary spectacle that no one interested in scientific curiosities will want to miss: one can observe the passage of the sun from within the building itself. This feature of the cathedral was restored to full "working order" in 1996 and now the ecclesiastical authorities, working in conjunction with a committee dedicated to promoting public interest in astronomy, allow groups to observe the phenomenon; in theory, these groups should be limited to 150 people, but there were 250 on the day we visited. What one sees is the sudden apparition of a circle of light which then can be observed moving across the floor to come to rest exactly over a circle of marble whose position was calculated in 1475 by Paolo dal Pozzo Toscanelli (1397-1482).

Apart from these special days, there is little visible trace of the astronomical activity associated with the church: the Capella della Croce is reserved for religious services, and the marks inlaid in the floor are hidden beneath a copper cover.

During the Renaissance, astronomers were allowed to take advantage of the internal layout of the cathedral and the exceptional height of its cupola to carry out measurements that previously had been impossible. Toscanelli had actually assisted Brunelleschi in his calculations regarding the cathedral dome, and in 1475 he was allowed to install below the windows of the lantern a bronze plaque (la bronzina) with an opening measuring about 5cm across. The ray of light that passed through this opening fell to the floor of the building in the Cappella della Croce; the exact spot where it strikes at the time of the summer solstice is marked by a marble disk that is still visible today. In 1510 this disk was enclosed within a wider circle, whose diameter corresponds more exactly to the diameter of the ray of sunlight as its hits the floor (the original was maintained out of respect for Toscanelli's work). This feature of the building was used in various types of astronomical work, including the reformation of the calendar. It has also served to study sun spots, the progression of eclipses, and the transit of Venus in front of the sun.

(N.B. For more information on how such meridians work, see the following double-page spread.)

THE XIMENES SUNDIAL ❷

Church of Santa Maria del Fiore

*An epic worthy
of a novel*

Church of Santa Maria del Fiore In 1754, almost 300 years after Toscanelli, Leonardo Ximenes (1716-1786) used the above-mentioned opening to calculate the variations in the angle of inclination of the Earth's axis with respects to the plane of its elliptical orbit. His proposal to use the specific characteristics of the building (the height of the cupola permitted unusually precise measurements) aroused the immediate interest of both civil and religious authorities.

In 1755 he obtained permission to have a marble meridian line inlaid on the floor of the Capella della Croce (this ran through the two previously installed marble disks). The calibrations on this line made it possible to read the angle of the solar image directly, with Ximenes' calculations finally concluding that the inclination of the Earth's axis changed by just over 30" (that is, about one fiftieth of a degree) per century. Modern-day astronomers put the figure at around 47".

For Ximenes, it was essential that the observational readings be "absolute," so that they could be "transferable." This meant that he had to be able to give the precise size of all the instruments he used – for example, the height of the gnomonic opening above the floor of the cathedral. In fact, near the high altar (but not open to visitors) there is an elliptical paving stone that indicates the point which forms an exact perpendicular with the central axis of that opening. Note that within the stone are engraved standard measures of a *braccio fiorentino* (58.36 cm) and a *pied parisien* (32.48 cm). Ximenes had to overcome considerable difficulties in order to obtain the necessary precision in his measurements of the opening's height. For example, to measure the vertical distance from the opening to the floor (just under 90 m) he used a copper chain. When this was suspended down to the floor, however, the links stretched. And even that stretching varied according to the weight the individual link was actually supporting (i.e. its position in the chain). This meant that when the chain was returned to the horizontal, it was no longer the same length. Ximenes therefore decided to measure it when suspended, using the standard measurement he chose for the purpose: the *toise parisienne* (1.95 m). Another problem was the expansion of this steel standard due to increases in temperature. If this was not to invalidate his observations, he had to carry out all the different measurements on the same day and at the same time, allowing for the fact that the temperature within the cathedral varies as one gets closer to the lantern. The error in his final measurements was no more than 2 per 100,000 – a remarkable degree of precision for that period.

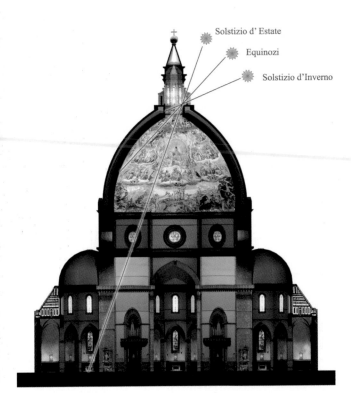

Solstizio d' Estate

Equinozi

Solstizio d'Inverno

HOW DOES A MERIDIAN WORK?

Instead of the using the shadow of a gnomon, these use a small hole placed at a certain height, through which the sun's light falls onto a meridian line (i.e. one aligned exactly north-south). The fact that the sun's rays perform the function of the shadow in a traditional sundial means that the opening is sometimes referred to as a "gnomonic opening." The higher the opening, the more efficient the meridian, hence the interest in using cathedrals (see the following section "Why are meridians installed in cathedrals?"); the circumference of the hole had to be no more than one thousandth of the height above the ground. Obviously, the opening had to be installed on the south side of the building in order to let in the rays of the sun, which lies to the south in the northern hemisphere.

The meridian line should run from the point which stands perpendicularly below the axis of the opening, not always easy to determine using the instruments available to scientists in the past (see "The Epic of Ximenes' Meridian"). The length of the line depends on the height of the opening; in some cases, where the building was not long enough to trace the entire meridian line across the floor (as was the case at Saint-Sulpice in Paris), an obelisk was added at its end, so that the movement of the sun's ray could then be measured up the vertical. In summer, when the sun is highest in the sky, the sun's ray falls onto the meridian line closer to the south wall (where that line begins) than it does in winter, when the sun is lower over the horizon and the rays tend to strike towards the far end of the meridian line.

The main principle behind the working of the meridian is that at noon, solar time, the sun is at its apex and, by definition, its rays fall straight along a line running exactly north-south. So, the exact moment when those rays strike the meridian line, which does run north-south, indicates the solar noon. Furthermore, the exact place on the meridian line where that ray falls makes it possible to determine the day of the year: the point right at the beginning of the line is reached solely on the day of the summer solstice, whilst the exact end of the line is reached on the day of the winter solstice. Experience and observation meant that the meridian line could be calibrated to identify different days of the year.

Once this was done, one could use the line to establish the date of various moveable feasts, such as Easter – one of the great scientific and religious uses of meridians. Similarly, one could establish the different periods corresponding with the signs of the Zodiac, which explains where one finds such signs indicated along the length of a number of meridian lines (see the Baptistery, page 33)

WHY WAS 4 OCTOBER FOLLOWED IMMEDIATELY BY 15 OCTOBER IN THE YEAR 1582?

THE MEASUREMENT OF TIME AND THE ORIGIN OF THE MERIDIANS

The entire problem of the measurement of time and the establishment of calendars arises from the fact that the Earth does not take an exact number of days to orbit the sun: one orbit in fact takes neither 365 nor 366 days but rather 365 days, 5 hours, 48 minutes and 45 seconds.

At the time of Julius Caesar, Sosigenes of Alexandria calculated this orbit as 365 days and 6 hours. In order to make up for this difference of an extra 6 hours, he came up with the idea of an extra day every four years: thus the Julian calendar – and the leap year – came into being.

In 325 AD, the Council of Nicaea established the temporal power of the Church (it had been called by Constantine, the first Roman emperor to embrace Christianity). The Church's liturgical year contained fixed feasts such as Christmas, but also moveable feasts such as Easter. This latter was of essential importance as it commemorated the death and resurrection of Christ, and so the Church decided that it should fall on the first Sunday following the full moon after the spring equinox. That year, the equinox fell on 21 March, which was thus established as its permanent date.

However, over the years, observation of the heavens showed that the equinox (which corresponds with a certain known position of the stars) no longer fell on 21 March...The 11 minutes and 15 seconds difference between the real and assumed time of the Earth's orbit around the Sun was resulting in an increasing gap between the actual equinox and 21 March. By the 16th century, that gap had increased to ten full days and so pope Gregory XIII decided to intervene. Quite simply, ten days would be removed from the calendar on 1582, and one would pass directly from 4 October to 15 October... It was also decided, on the basis of complex calculations (carried out most notably by the Calabrian astronomer Luigi Giglio), that the first year of each century (ending in 00) would not actually be a leap year, even though divisible by four. The exceptions would fall every four hundred years, which would mean that in 400 years there would be a total of just 97 (rather than 100) leap years. This came closest to making up the shortfall resulting from difference between the real and assumed time of orbit. Thus 1700, 1800 and 1900 would not be leap years, but 2000 would...

In order to establish the full credibility of this new calendar – and convince the various Protestant nations that continued to use the Julian calendar – Rome initiated the installation of large meridians within its churches. A wonderful scientific epic had begun...

The technical name for a leap year is a bissextile year. The term comes from the fact that the additional day was once placed between 24 and 25 February. In Latin, 24 February was the sixth (sextus) day before the calends of March, hence the name *bis sextus*, to indicate a supplementary sixth day. The calends were the first day of each month in the Roman calendar.

THE MERIDIAN OF SANTA MARIA DEL FIORE: THE HIGHEST MERIDIAN IN THE WORLD

From the 15th to the 18th century almost 70 meridians were installed in churches in France and Italy. Only ten, however, have a gnomonic opening that is more than 10 metres above floor level – that height being crucial to the accuracy of the instrument:

S. Maria del Fiore (Florence)	90.11 m
S. Petronio (Bologna)	27.07 m
St-Sulpice (Paris)	26.00 m
Monastery of San Nicolo l'Arena (Catania, Sicily)	23.92 m
Cathedral (Milan)	23.82 m
S. Maria degli Angeli (Rome)	20.34 m
Collège de l'Oratoire (Marseille)	17.00 m
S. Giorgio (Modica, Sicily)	14.18 m
Museo Nazionale (Naples)	14.00 m
Cathedral (Palermo)	11.78 m

WHY WERE MERIDIANS INSTALLED IN CATHEDRALS

To make their measurements more precise, astronomers required enclosed spaces where the point admitting light was as high as possible from the ground: the longer the beam of light, the more accurately they could establish that it was meeting the floor along an exactly perpendicular plane. Cathedrals were soon recognised as the ideal location for such scientific instruments as meridians. Furthermore, the Church had a vested interest as well, because meridians could be used to establish the exact date of Easter.

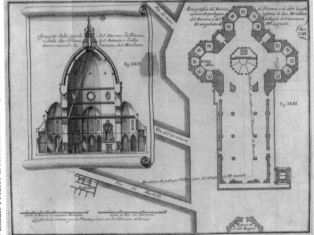

© Istituto e Museo di Storia della Scienza, Firenze

THE CATHEDRAL WINDLASS ❸

Piazza del Duomo
50122 Florence (FI)
• Access to the cupola: Monday to Friday 8.30-19.00, Saturday 8.30-17.40. First Saturday of the month, 8.30-16.00. Closed Sunday and holidays. Last admission: 40 minutes before closing time.
• Admission: 6 €.
• Note: There are 463 steps to climb.

The last vestiges of the building work on the original cathedral

Designed and built by Filippo Brunelleschi in 1420-1436, the cupola of Florence cathedral is a masterpiece known worldwide. One of the oddities of the project was that no previous designs had been put forward for the covering of the crossing and choir. Given the immense size involved*, innovative techniques were required, both in the design of the cupola and in the methods used to raise thousands of tons of building materials up to this great height.

Brunelleschi gave further proof of his technical genius in resolving this engineering problem, inventing lifting equipment whose gear systems greatly increased the force exerted. His skill in mechanics came from the knowledge of clock-making acquired whilst studying as a goldsmith. Ten years later, the machinery he designed would again prove its usefulness when it served to raise the sphere atop the lantern, an operation in which the young Leonardo da Vinci also played a part (see below, on the collapse of the lantern in 1600). There are only a few humble remains of this splendid building equipment, including two modest windlasses made of wood; they hang beneath the central vaults of two of the four "blank galleries" (those to the south side of the cupola). Located on the outside of the choir walls, under the oculi, these galleries form small bulges which apparently serve no purpose. In fact, Brunelleschi designed them to reinforce the existing structure onto which his cupola would repose.

SIGHTS NEARBY:

THE MARK COMMEMORATING THE COLLAPSE OF THE CATHEDRAL LANTERN ❹

To the rear of the cathedral there is a round marble plaque inlaid in the grey paving stones. There is no inscription to indicate that it was placed here to commemorate the collapse of the lantern on 17 February 1600. The fall was the result of lightning striking the gilded copper sphere (weight: more than 2 tonnes) which had adorned its summit. The work of Verrocchio, the lantern had been set in place in 1468, in part thanks to machinery specially designed by Leonardo da Vinci. Restored, it was again set in place in 1602 – but this time protected by a lightning conductor.

---

* The cupola stands some 35.5m in height above its drum. This means that it rises to about 90 m above floor level (107m if one includes the lantern). It is estimated to weigh around 37,000 tonnes.

THE BULL OF THE PORTA DELLA MANDORLA

The Porta della Mandorla gives access to the massive cupola designed by Brunelleschi; there are 463 steps up from the inner gallery. Among the sculptures adorning that doorway is a bull's head with a fine set of horns, which seems to be looking leftwards at the house opposite. The bull is said to have been put in this place by a mocking stonemason. A clear reference to the horns of cuckoldry, it stands directly opposite the windows of a man who was jealous of his beautiful young wife.

THE PORTA DEI LEONI AND A NIGHTMARE

The other doorway on the north side of the cathedral is flanked by two columns bearing a lion and a lioness. Known as Porta Balla, it is also called Porta dei Cornacchini after a tragic event that is said to have taken place in the 15th century. Anselmo, a neighbour of the Cornacchini family, one night had a terrible nightmare that he was being devoured by the lion that stood atop this doorway column. The next day, to exorcise this nightmare, he went up to the lion and stuck his hand in its open jaw. Unfortunately, in doing so he disturbed a fat scorpion that was nesting there. Poor Anselmo died from the sting that same day.

DANTE'S AMAZING MEMORY

Opposite the south wall of the cathedral, beneath the house number at 54 Piazza del Duomo, a plaque commemorates that this was the site of "Dante's Stone," the lump of rock on which the poet used to sit while watching work on the cathedral. It is also said that this was the site of an amusing incident that illustrates the poet's quite amazing memory. A passer-by stopped one day behind him and asked "Hey, Dante! What is your favourite food?" "Eggs," the poet replied. One year later the man was passing by the same spot and decided to put to test the poet's memory: "What with?" he asked. "Salt,' Dante answered, without even turning round.

SIGHTS NEARBY:

SURREPTITIOUS SELF-PORTRAIT OF GIUSEPPE CASSIOLI ❺

Cathedral of Florence
Piazza del Duomo
50122 Florence (FI)

• Opening hours: Monday to Wednesday, Friday 10.00-17.00, Thursday 10.00-15.30, Saturday 10.00-16.45, Sunday and holidays 13.30-16.45.
• Free admission

Six centuries after the laying of the first stone, the façade of the Cathedral of Santa Maria dei Fiori was officially unveiled on 12 March 1887. Ten years later, the door in the left portal of the façade was completed by Augusto Passaglia. And twelve years after that, the door on the right was completed by the brothers Amos and Giuseppe Cassioli.

In response to insistent criticisms of his delay in finishing the work, Giuseppe Cassioli would actually depict himself in the bronze, being strangled by a serpent. The self-portrait is to the right of the door, at about eye level.

The central doors, again the work of Augusto Passaglia, were officially unveiled in 1903 by King Vittorio-Emanuele III, thus marking the end to work on the cathedral's façade.

SIGHTS NEARBY:

THE BISCHERI INSCRIPTION ❻

On the south side of the cathedral, near the bell tower, is an inscription just above eye level to the right of the visitors' doorway. Carved into marble, this announces the birth of a member of the Bischieri family. Due to the history of the Bischieri, the word has in Tuscan dialect become a synonym for "idiot."

When planning to build the cathedral, the authorities of the Republic of Florence had to expropriate the homes of those who lived on the selected site. Each householder was offered a reasonable price; however, the Bischieri family refused point blank and would not budge. It is said that a mysterious fire then destroyed the houses that they owned, and thus they received only a derisory sum in compensation for their now-vacant plot. Another version has it that the Florentine authorities lost patience with them and exiled the entire family without compensation. Hence the use of their name to indicate someone who is stupid and pigheaded. Hence also the fact that the family preferred to change their name to Guadagni [Earnings]...

Where Via dell'Oriulo runs into Piazza del Duomo there is a plaque with the inscription *Canto dei Bischieri* [Bischieri Corner]; it indicates where the family used to live.

SIGHTS NEARBY:

A CONCEALED SELF-PORTRAIT OF GHIBERTI

The Baptistery's "Porta del Paradiso"

Piazza del Duomo

50122 Florence (FI)

Lorenzo Ghiberti's masterpiece, the bronze doors to the Baptistery — which Michelangelo christened La Porta del Paradiso — contain a hidden portrait of the bald artist looking rather sly. This is to be found on the frame itself, at the fifth level of individual scenes; these scenes are to be read left to right — across both doors - from the top downwards. At the same level, on the right door, there is also a portrait of Bartoluccio, Ghiberti's teacher and father-in-law.

The doors to the Baptistery are so heavy that, as Galileo observed, even if you exerted only the slightest force in closing them, they would make the entire building shake when they banged shut.

Around the doorway, the two broken columns of porphyry seem to be placed there by chance. In fact, they were a gift from the city of Pisa, in thanks for Florence's aid in war against the city of Lucca in 1117. Though damaged during transport, they were nevertheless set in place so as not to offend the donors.

RECYCLED BUILDING STONE

Like a number of cathedrals, most notably perhaps that of Pisa, the Florence Baptistery made ample use of building stones from elsewhere, some of them already sculpted. To the left of the north doorway, almost at ground level, the sharp-eyed will be able to make out a sculpted frieze; depicting a naval scene with various figures, this probably came from the side of a Roman sarcophagus. More recycled building material can be seen to the top-right of the east doorway (that facing the cathedral), where a curious inscription is embedded in the wall.

TRACES OF OLD STANDARDS OF MEASUREMENT IN THE BAPTISTERY

8

Piazza del Duomo
50122 Florence (FI)

Curious rectangles are engraved in the stone of the columns flanking the south door of the Baptistery. On the left-hand column there are two, one inside the other; their purpose is today unknown. On the right-hand column there is a single larger rectangle that provides the standard measure of the "Lombard foot."

> *Before the metre, the arms and legs of monarchs served as standard measures...*

Originally introduced by king Liutprand (690?-744), the piede lombardo would undergo the same changes as other units of measurement and ultimately vary from city to city and century to century, ranging from 38 to 51.5 cm. Its original introduction had been part of measures intended to unify Italy under Lombard rule that were not always well-received and often opposed by the papacy.

It is said that Liutprand was exceptionally tall for the period - 1.73 m - and that his right foot measured 25.4 cm and his right 26.1, making the sum of the two royal feet 51.5cm. These very precise figures have been disproved thanks to the identification of Liutprand's remains in the church of San Pietro in Ciel d'Oro in Pavia, the Lombard capital. In fact, the king seems to have been of normal height for his times.

Still, some thousand years after his reign, his foot was still being used as a unit of measurement in some Italian cities...

WHAT PRECEDED THE METRIC SYSTEM?

On 28 July 1861 Italy officially adopted the metric system. Before that, each province – or even city – had its own units of measurement, sometimes based upon the size of a monarch's foot or arm or hand. This confusion explains why such standards were often displayed in public places, primarily markets, where vendors and customers could consult them. Some of these old units of measurement can still be seen in Volterra (see page 129) and Barga (see page 205).

In Florence, the most commonly used units were the *braccio fiorentino* (58.4 cm) and the *canna agrimensoria* (2.92 m). The Florentine foot (*piede fiorentino*) was the same length as the *pied parisien* (32.48 cm). This latter had become something of a standard measure throughout Europe thanks to the renown enjoyed by the architects of France's Gothic cathedrals.

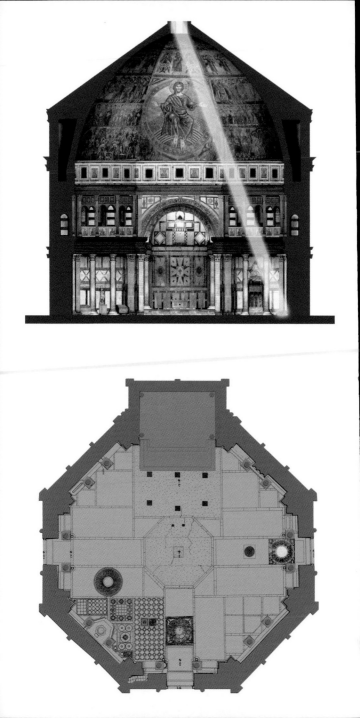

THE BAPTISTERY PALINDROME

9

Piazza del Duomo
50122 Florence (FI)
Opening hours: 12.15-19.00, Sunday and holidays 8.30-14.00. Closed 1 January,
Easter, 8 September and Christmas Day.
Admission: 3 €

> *A solar palindrome; the remains of the meridian in the Baptistery*

Between the north and east doors of the Baptistery, the floor is embellished with a circle of the zodiac. Around the sun at the centre is inscribed this Latin palindrome* en giro torte sol ciclos et rotor igne [I am the sun. I am this wheel moved by fire, whose turning turns the spheres]. This circle is, in fact, the remains of a sundial which stood in this spot before the year 1000 AD. Built between the 4th and 5th centuries AD, the Baptistery would become a Christian building around the 7th century, serving as a cathedral until 1128, when it officially became a baptistery. A hole in the cupola allowed in a ray light which, according to the time of year, illuminated one of the signs of the zodiac placed at the edge of the baptistery's walls. In the 13th century, a new marble floor – identical to the old one – was laid. However, as Filippo Villani (1325-1407) explains in his Chronicles, the renovators did not respect the original position of the signs because for at least three centuries the solar clock had no longer worked properly: the precession of the equinoxes** had made the meridian increasingly inaccurate. So the opening in the cupola was filled in and the circle of the zodiac on the floor became merely a decorative feature.

* A palindrome is a phrase, word or number that is identical whether read from left to right or right to left.

** The precession of the equinoxes is the slow shift backwards of the equinoctial points along the elliptic. This is due to the slow change in the axis of the Earth's rotation, forming a sort of conical oscillation which takes about 25,800 years to complete.

Racroglie grerco   e xualto   Stimolato dal
el a uolo

Lo   Conducono   in   piatenta   Lo

SIGNIO
GIESVC
TOABI
RICHC
DELAN
MIA

THE PUNISHMENT OF THE "FOULER" OF TABERNACLESS **⑩**

Church of Santa Maria de' Ricci
Via del Corso
Museo Stibbert - 26, Via Federico Stibbert
• Tel: 055 475520 • Opening hours: Monday to Wednesday 10.00-14.00, Friday to
Sunday 10.00-18.00.
Admission: 5 €, reduced: 2 €.

A 16th century cartoon strip

Standing practically opposite the entrance to Vicolo del Panico, the church of Santa Maria de' Ricci contains (in the last chapel on the left) a reproduction of a painting that is divided into nine different compartments, rather like a period "cartoon strip." The work recounts the construction of this church dedicated to the Virgin Mary, and how it was built in reparation for a grave act of sacrilege that had taken place on 21 July 1501. Having lost all his money one evening playing at dice at the Albergo del Fico, Antonio di Giovanni Rinaldeschi was going home when he passed by a tabernacle with a depiction of the Annunciation. In his anger at his losses, he picked up a lump of horse dung and threw it in the Virgin's face, much to the horror of those present. Taken to the Bargello*, the man was then hung from the window of the building after a very perfunctory trial. While the Annunciation that was the object of the defilement can still be seen in the choir of the church of Santa Maria de' Ricci, the original of the "cartoon strip" is now in the Museo Stibbert, where its full glory can now be appreciated thanks to recent restoration.

* The Bargello was the palace of the *podestà* or city governor/magistrate. Built in the 13th-14th century, it was originally home to the *capitano del popolo*, the head of the local militia, but from the middle of the 14th century became the seat of the *podestà*, who was head of both the executive and judiciary. Only in 1574 did it become the *Palazzo del Bargello* [chief of police], being transformed into a prison where suspects were interrogated and executions performed. Today, the Bargello is a museum dedicated primarily to Italian Renaissance sculpture.

SIGHTS NEARBY:
PANIC ALLEY **⑪**

Vicolo del Panìco - From Via del Corso to Via Dante Alighieri
49r, Via del Corso. 8, Via Dante Alighieri - 50122 Florence (FI)
Even if it is often omitted from maps, the old Vicolo del Panico still exists, running from a gated opening at 49r Via del Corso to 8 Via Dante Alighieri, where stands the poet's house.
The history associated with this alley is an amazing one. After the victory of the Guelphs over the Ghibellines, the Guelph party itself split due to a power struggle between two groups: on the one hand were the Cerchi family and the "White Guelphs" (who were more populist), on the other the Donati family and the "Black Guelphs" (members of the Florentine elite). Those living in the same neighbourhood often found themselves living right next door to families that were now their enemies. This proximity made it possible to sneak into an enemy's house through the adjoining wall. To prevent such intrusions, the municipal authorities decided to order the demolition of walls that presented this risk, thus creating new public footpaths that were not on existing maps.

THE FACE OF LA BERTA

⑫

Church of Santa Maria Maggiore
Piazza Santa Maria Maggiore

> **The mysterious face outside Santa Maria Maggiore**

Passing from Via de' Cerratani alongside the north side of Santa Maria Maggiore, you have to look carefully to see this curious face, which stares outwards without deigning to look down. According to some, its origin dates back to 1327, when the astrologer Francesco Stabili (better known as Cecco d'Ascoli) was condemned to be burnt at the stake. Before the execution, a priest claimed to know of the pact the astrologer had made with the Devil, who had apparently promised Francesco that he would be safe from all perils if he drank a sip of water. "Whatever you do, do not give him anything to drink!" the priest shouted. To which the condemned man replied: *E tu il capo de lì non caverà mai* ["You'll never get that out of your head" or "Your head will never get out of that'"]. And thus the priest's head can still be seen where it turned to stone at that very moment.

Another story has it that a woman from the countryside who brought vegetables to market had given the parish a clock so that those who did not live in the city could have ample warning of the closure of the city gates (or, according to another version, so that the gates could be opened for those who were late). The Florentines are said to have commissioned a sculpture of this generous donor and had it installed here.

But there is also a third story. A condemned man on his way to execution cursed a woman who was mocking him. Her head immediately turned to stone, and was thrown up to the place where it can still be seen today...

THE LITTLE DEVIL

⓭

Corner of Via degli Strozzi and Via de' Vecchietti

> *Satan on horseback*

On the corner of Palazzo Vecchietti at the junction of Via degli Strozzi and Via de' Vecchietti is a bronze statue of an insolent, jeering little devil. The work of Giambologna (or Jean de Boulogne, Douai, 1529 – Florence, 1608), it was commissioned by Bernardo Vecchietti to commemorate a mysterious incident in Florence's history.

In 1425 a Dominican friar, Pietro da Verona (see below), a sort of precursor of Savonarola, was preaching against heresy in Piazza del Mercato Vecchio (now Piazza della Repubblica) when a startled black horse ran into the square. The monk, immediately realising that this was a ruse of the Devil to distract his listeners, raised his hand to make a large sign of the cross over the satanic beast. The possessed beast withdrew and disappeared around the corner of Palazzo Vecchietti, leaving nothing but a plume of smoke and a strong smell of sulphur...

PIETRO DA VERONA

Pietro da Verona, also known as St. Peter Martyr, was born in Verona in 1205 to a Cathar family. Having become a Dominican, he gained a reputation for his visceral opposition to heretical ideas and was appointed head inquisitor for Lombardy, where he became known for the number of victims he condemned to burn at the stake. When he later moved to Florence, he established a sort of Christian militia to fight against the Patarini, a movement of clergy and populace rebelling against the excesses of certain prelates and their way of life.* It is said that he feared his life would come to violent end due to the hatred he aroused. And that is what happened on 6 April 1252, when a certain Pietro da Balsamo split his head open with a billhook; the murderer later repented his crime and himself became a Dominican. In the numerous paintings of this murder, one sees the saint almost impervious to the cleaver buried in his skull. Only two years after his death, the man was canonised as St. Peter Martyr by Pope Innocent IV, who thus exalted the role he had played in fighting heresy.

* Two violent clashes are said to have occurred during the year 1244. Historians nowadays have cast doubts on such stories, even if there are two columns in Florence that were raised to commemorate these events: one, La Colonna della Croce al Trebbio, stands at the corner of Via del Moro, Via delle Belle Donne and Via del Trebbio, the other, La Colonna Santa Felicità, stands in the square of the same name.

THE WINE COUNTERS (BUCHETTE) IN FLORENTINE PALAZZI

Palazzo Viviani, 2, Via delle Belle Donne

2, Via del Giglio

Hotel Monna Lisa. 27, Borgo Pinti

Renaissance winesellers

Beside the main entrances to Florentine palazzi one sometimes finds small shutters in the wall. These are a curiosity typical of the city, even if the feature does occur elsewhere: for example, Volterra (6, Via Buonparenti) and Colle di Val d'Elsa (14, Via Campana). Known as buchette, these shutters enclosed counters where important Florentine families could sell the wine they produced.

Each counter had its own opening times, generally on a weekly basis. Bottled at the vineyard, the wine was delivered from the country in flasks with a narrow neck and wide bottom, which were protected by being encased in straw (just like some Chianti bottles).

One of the most interesting of these wine counters is the one at Palazzo Viviani at 2, Via Delle Belle Donne (the name stems not so much from the beauty of the women there as from their promiscuity). The opening hours, according to season, are still engraved on a stone tablet: 1 November to April, 9.00-14.00 and 17.00-18.00; 1 May to October, 8.00-15.00 and 8.00-9.00. On holidays the counter closed at 15.00.

The finest buchetta is undoubtedly that at 2, Via del Giglio: the opening is in the form of an actual doorway in a rusticated façade similar to ones found on numerous Florentine palazzi. The marble plaque to the upper left of the palazzo doorway still bears the counter's opening hours. These are slightly later that those for the Via delle Belle Donne wine counter, which seems logical given that the owners of this palazzo, the Bartolini Salimbeni, had as their family motto Per non Dormire [so as not to sleep]; it is actually inscribed on their palazzo in Piazza Santa Trinità.

At 27 Borgo Pinti, the Hotel Monna Lisa has another wine counter, this one located within the antechamber to the building, which was readily accessible to the public. While the present owners may have hidden the actual opening behind a massive plant, the niche itself, along with the two sills where the wine bottles were placed, makes it easy to understand how this small but flourishing outlet must have worked.

TO FIND OUT MORE:
Le buchette del vino a Firenze, Lidia Casini Brogelli, Edizioni Semper.

ARMILLARY SPHERE IN THE CHURCH OF SANTA MARIA NOVELLA ⑮

Church of Santa Maria Novella
Piazza di Santa Maria Novella

The sphere at the origin of the Gregorian calendar

Ignazio Danti, a Dominican monk who was also an astronomer and cartographer, included two astronomical instruments in the façade of the church of Santa Maria Novella. To the right of the entrance is a marble gnomon*, to the left a bronze armillary sphere (see below). It was with these instruments that Friar Danti calculated the discrepancy between the solar year and the Julian calendar, which had been devised by Julius Caesar in 46 BC, promulgated by law the following year and had remained in force ever since.

Having persuaded Pope Gregory XIII to recognise the importance of his calculations, the Dominican scholar then formed part of a committee of scientists (headed by Christophorus Calvius) which would successfully argue for the introduction of the new, "Gregorian" , calendar. As already mentioned, the realignment involved skipping ahead ten days, so that one passed directly from 4 October 1582 to 15 October 1582 (see above and page 22).

THE JULIAN CALENDAR
The Julian calendar, developed during the reign of Julius Caesar (hence the name), remained in force until the reform introduced by Pope Gregory XIII in 1582. The Gregorian calendar which takes its name from that pope introduced a reform in the counting of leap years, which had previously meant that the date indicated by the calendar fell further and further behind the solar date. The most spectacular effect of the introduction the new calendar was, in fact the suppression of ten days. And this is why St. Theresa of Avila died on the night between 4 October and 15 October 1582...

ARMILLARY SPHERE
An armillary sphere or spherical astrolabe is a representation of the sphere of the heavens showing the movement of the stars around the Earth or sun. The name comes from the Latin for 'bracelet', given that such a sphere is made up of concentric calibrated circles which show the revolutions of celestial objects. Armillary spheres were developed by the Greeks and were already being used in the 2nd century BC, most notably by Ptolemy.

* A gnomon is the upright on a sundial whose shadow is cast onto a flat surface.

THE "STENDHAL SYNDROME"

From Northern Europe, America, Africa and Asia, art lovers arrive in Florence after years of knowing its masterpieces only through books and reproductions. Almost without any period of transition, they find themselves looking at Botticelli's paintings, Michelangelo's sculptures, Brunelleschi's cupola and Ghiberti's doors for the Baptistery. Suddenly, there they are: the masterpieces of the Italian Renaissance! ... And a veil seems to fall before the enthusiast's eye... The beauty is too much and causes the heart to race; it becomes a hallucination, a source of dizziness. Swooning can turn to fainting, and an ambulance has to be called out... The phenomenon has long been recognised and even has a name: the "Stendhal Syndrome."

The hospital of Santa Maria Nuova, in Piazza Santa Maria Nuova, actually has a special service for treating those who fall victim to the impact of a close encounter with "the real thing." Graziella Magherini, a psychiatrist and psychoanalyst who long worked in the psychiatric ward of the hospital, was the one who invented the name, taking it as the title of a book which she dedicated to the malaise which works of art can cause in some people.

The expression was inspired by the fact that the French writer Stendhal (Marie-Henri Beyle) would mention feeling such "symptoms" when visiting Florence in 1817. This is how he describes his visit to the church of Santa Croce and his reaction to the sight of Volterrano's frescoes and of the tombs of Michelangelo, Alfieri and Galileo: "I was already in a sort of ecstasy at the mere idea of being in Florence... Absorbed in the contemplation of sublime beauty, I was seeing it close-to, I was, one might say, touching it. I was at that point where the celestial sensations caused by the fine arts encounter the power of the passions. Upon leaving Santa Croce, I felt my heart racing. I walked as if I was afraid of collapsing."

There are other cities where such reactions have been noted, particularly Jerusalem and Paris. In the latter, for example, Japanese tourists, already disturbed by the pushing and shoving in the Metro, feel something similar on finding that the Eiffel Tower is so much smaller than they had imagined it.

It should be pointed out that some doctors argue that the syndrome is nothing more than the result of blood failing to reach the brain because people are continually tilting their head to see painted ceilings and other works above eye-level....

Hospital of Santa Maria Nuova. Piazza Santa Maria Nuova. Tel: 055 27581. Emergency Services number: 118.

PALAZZO MEDICI RICCARDI

3, Via Cavour

16

A large number of the stones in the rustication of the imposing Palazzo Medici Riccardi are marked with a circle. This was the quarry mark used by the architect, Michelozzo di Bartolomeo Michelozzi (known as Michelozzo), to indicate stones suitable for use on this façade effect.

Michelozzo's mark in palazzo Medici Riccardi

WHY WAS THE WINDOW AT THE FAR RIGHT OF PALAZZO PUZZI BRICKED UP DURING THE 16TH CENTURY?

Closely linked with the Medici, the Pucci family had profited from this alliance throughout the 15th century – that is, up to 1560, when Cosimo I banished Pandolfo de' Pucci from his court. Pandolfo then hired assassins to kill the Grand Duke. They were to fire on Cosimo with arquebuses when he passed in front of Palazzo Pucci on his way to the basilica in Piazza Santissima Annunziata. But the plot was unmasked and Pandolfo was caught and then hung from a window of the Bargello. As a lasting visible reminder of that punishment, and perhaps to exorcise the evil intentions associated with the building, Cosimo had the window on the far right of the palace's ground floor bricked up.

Palazzo Pucci. Via de' Pucci, 2.

THE CYLINDER OF THE OSPEDALE DEGLI INNOCENTI

Piazza della Santissima Annunziata

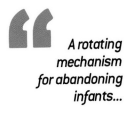

A rotating mechanism for abandoning infants...

I n Piazza della Santissima Annunziata stands the Ospedale degli Innocenti which once functioned as an orphanage for foundlings and abandoned children. So that infants could be left at any hour of the night, there was a special system installed by the doorway at the end of the arcade in front of the building. At the bottom of a false doorway was a rotating cylinder into which one could place the infant through the outer opening. The small cord alongside was atta-ched to a bell which told those inside that an infant had just been left. Apart from the rotating cylinder itself, everything is just as it was on 5 February 1445, when the institution received its first "innocent," a girl, who was then named Agata after the saint whose feast day fell on that date. Also known to the Florentines as "the crib," the "foundlings' wheel" would remain in use until 1875.

To facilitate the adoption of these foundlings – or perhaps allow remorseful parents to take them back– the infants were put on public display within the Loggia del Bigallo, near the Cathedral.

THE FOUNDLINGS' WHEEL

It is said that in 787, Dateus, a priest in Milan, began placing a large bas-ket outside his church so that abandoned infants could be left there. More organised initiatives for the reception of abandoned children were begun by the Hospice des Chanoines in Marseilles from 1188 onwards, with Pope Innocent III (1198-1216) later giving the practice the Church's benediction; he had been horrified by the terrible sight of the bodies of abandoned infants floating in the Tiber and was determined to do some-thing to save them. So the doors of convents were equipped with a sort of rotating cradle which made it possible for parents to leave their infant anonymously and without exposing them to the elements. The infant was left in the outside section of the cradle, and then the parent rang a bell so that the nuns could activate the mechanism and bring the child inside. Access to the "turntable" was, however, protected by a grill so narrow that only newborn infants would fit through... Abandoned during the 19th century, the system has, over the last twenty years, had to be re-adopted at various places in Europe due to the sharp upturn in the number of infants abandoned, primarily by immigrant women who have no means to support them.

THE BEES OF FERDINANDO I

18

Piazza della Santissima Annunziata

A swarm of bees

This equestrian statue of Ferdinand 1, Grand Duke of Tuscany from 1587 to 1609, is the work of Giambologna; it was cast from the bronze of Turkish cannons captured by the Knights of Santo Stefano. On one side of the monument is the sovereign's curious symbol: a queen bee surrounded by concentric circles of worker bees.

Tradition has it that it will bring you good luck if you manage to count all the bees without touching or marking them in any way. There are between 90 and 110…

The queen bee and the drones are said to symbolise the grand duke surrounded by the hard-working people of Tuscany.

SIGHTS NEARBY:

A WINDOW IN PALAZZO GRIFONI THAT NEVER CLOSES

19

Piazza della Santissima Annunziata

The window on the right of the second floor of Palazzo Grifoni is known as "the window that never closes;" in fact, the shutters are always ajar. It is said that from here a woman of the Grifoni family waved her last farewell to her husband as he departed for war. She then watched here for his return, but he never came back. When she died, someone went to close the window. One story goes that when he did this, the entire room became haunted, with paintings falling from the walls, furniture moving, and lamps going out. But everything went back to normal once the window was opened again.

Another tradition has it that it was the local residents who protested, as they had become accustomed to seeing the window ajar.

MICHELANGELO'S BUSYBODY

Piazza della Signoria

> *A very curious portrait...*

To the far right of the Palazzo Vecchio, the sharp-eyed will see – right behind the sculpture of Hercules and Cacus – a face carved into the stone, just above the bench on which tourists sit. This portrait is said to be the work of Michelangelo, created in circumstances about which there are two, equally surprising, versions.

One tells how Michelangelo was constantly being disturbed by a busybody who bored him about all sorts of pointless things. One day the busybody happened along while the sculptor had hammer and chisel in hand, so Michelangelo carved the man's portrait in the stone while pretending to listen to him. This would explain why the carving is known as L'Importuno by Florentines.

Another version has it that, present one day when a man was brought for execution in front of the palazzo, Michelangelo suddenly decided to make a portrait of the unfortunate wretch. Given he had little time, and wanted to keep his eye fixed on his subject, he had no other choice than to carve in the stone immediately behind him.

IS THERE A DA VINCI FRESCO HIDDEN IN THE PALAZZO VECCHIO?

Commissioned by the governors of Florence to decorate one wall of the Chamber of the Council of Five Hundred in the Palazzo Vecchio, Leonardo's This would explain why the portrait does not have a high finish yet, with great economy of means, still gives a vivid impression of a personality.fresco *The Battle of Anghiari* still gives rise to talk. Having disappeared in rather mysterious circumstances, the work divides scholars. Most accept that it was painted on plaster that dried too quickly, and thus deteriorated so much that when Vasari was commissioned to renovate the decoration of the room, he painted over it. A smaller group argue that Vasari would never have taken such a cavalier attitude to the work of the master artist he admired above all others. What he did, in fact, was to install a brick wall just a few centimetres in front of the old fresco. The supporters of this theory claim that the words *Cerca, Trova* [search, find] which appear on the standard painted in Vasari's own fresco are a cryptic message.

THE "SCANDAL STONE"   **21**

Piazza del Mercato Nuovo

> **The backsides
> of the insolvent
> thumped against
> this stone**

During the day it is difficult to see the pietra dello scandalo that stands right at the centre of the Loggia del Mercato Nuovo: the place is packed with stalls selling souvenirs and leatherwear. You have to come here before 11 in the morning or after 8 in the evening. The spot is marked by an engraved marble wheel with six spokes. During the Middle Ages, it is said, this was where the Carroccio* (see page 111) was kept after a battle. Later, the stone was used as the place for the public humiliation of debtors and bankrupts. The punishment consisted in the culprit being chained to the spot, then his trousers were lowered and he was made to thump his bare arse on the engraving on the ground. This humiliating treatment is said to be the origin of a colloquial Italian way of saying "to go bankrupt" batter il culo sul lastrone [bash your arse on the paving].

SIGHTS NEARBY:

SCALES IN THE FARMACIA DEL CINGHIALE [THE WILD BOAR PHARMACY]   **22**
4r, Piazza del Mercato Nuovo
• Tel: 055 21 42 21
• Normal opening hours: 9.00-13.00 and 15.30-20.00. When the establishment acts as the "duty pharmacy" for the district, opening hours are different.
In Piazza del Mercato Nuovo, this historic pharmacy takes its name from the statue of a wild boar; tourists often caress the snout of this beast which itself accounts for the loggia sometimes being referred to as the Loggia del Porcellino (but this "piglet" is definitely a boar). The statue you can see today is a copy of the 1612 original by Pietro Tacca which is now in Palazzo Pitti (that work itself was a copy of a Greek marble original to be found in the Uffizi).
Founded at the beginning of the 18th century, the chemist's shop has since undergone a number of alterations, the most sizeable as a result of the floods of 1966. The most spectacular survivor of the old interior are the scales, in which a person can be weighed whilst comfortably seated in a copy of a Roman chair.

---

* The Carroccio was the four-wheeled chariot carrying the city standards around which the local militia formed themselves in battle (see page 111).

IL 4 NOVEMBRE 1966 L'ACQUA
D'ARNO ARRIVÒ A QUEST'ALTEZZA

PLAQUES INDICATING FLOOD LEVELS IN 1333 AND 1966 ㉓

Corner of Via de' Neri and Via San Remigio
50122 Florence (FI)

The city
under water

Right at the beginning of Via San Remigio, at the corner with Via de' Neri, you actually have to look up to see the two plaques that mark the level the waters reached in two different floods caused when the river Arno burst its banks. The two events were some 600 years apart, as you can see from the inscriptions: 4.92 m above ground level, the highest reads: "On 4 November 1966, the waters of the Arno reached this height," and just below is one that says, "On Thursday 4 November 1333 until the following Friday, the waters came up to here."

Of all the floods that Florence has suffered, that in 1966 remains the worst, causing 35 deaths and leaving some 100,000 Florentines trapped on rooftops or upper storeys for a whole day and night. The damage caused was immense: not only were some 15,000 cars carried away by the floodwaters, but when the doors of the church of Ognissanti gave way under the pressure, a tidal wave of mud poured into the building, soaking Botticelli's fresco of St. Augustine, painted in the 15th century. Elsewhere, at the church of Santa Croce, the tombs of Michelangelo, Galileo, Rossini and Machiavelli were submerged under 4.50 m of water. And as for the Uffizi, there the waters reached up to the third floor. Miraculously, all the city's bridges survived the catastrophe.

WINDOWS FOR CHILDREN

Finestrelle were small windows designed to allow children to look into the street without any danger of falling out. Placed just below normal windows, they were small in size and protected by bars. You can see several examples as you walk around Florence; all you have to do is glance up from time to time. The following are buildings where these characteristic *finestrelle* are still clearly visible:

• 3, Via del Corno. Just behind the Palazzo Vecchio.
• 8, Borgo Santa Croce. Next to Santa Croce, in the house where Vasari had his studio.
• 7r, Borgo San Frediano. In the district of Oltrarno, on the other side of the river.

FLORENTINE FOOTBALL

(24)

Palazzo degli Antellesi (20, Piazza Santa Croce) and at
7, Piazza Santa Croce

> *The markers of the halfway line can still be seen*

I n Piazza Santa Croce one can still see two traces of the pitch used for the old-style matches of calcio fiorentino. Dating from the Renaissance, the two markers indicated the ends of the halfway line of the field on which the matches were played. The first, bearing the date 10 February 1565, is a marble disk inlaid into the façade of Palazzo degli Antellesi (to the right as you look at the church; the marker has a jewellery shop to its right). The second, directly opposite at number 7, is smaller and divided into four quarters, two red, two white (they symbolise the ball used). A white line was traced on the ground between these two markers and served to divide the pitch into two equal halves occupied by the teams. It was from the centre point of that line that the referee (the pallaio) kicked the ball against one of the wall disks; when it fell back into play, the game commenced.

The noise and disturbance caused by Florentine football often annoyed many residents and one can see a number of wall plaques inscribed with prohibitions and restrictions:

Undated plaque at 1, Via Scala, prohibiting any sort of game.

Undated plaque in Via Alighieri, prohibiting all ballgames.

Undated plaque at 12, Via Magazzini, prohibiting all ballgames.

Plaque dated 1613 under the Loggia dei Servi in Piazza SS. Annunziata, prohibiting any sort of game within the loggia.

Plaque dated 1636 at 34, Via Colonna, prohibiting any sort of game.

Plaque dated 1646 in Via Bardi, at the church of S. Lucia, prohibiting all games inside the church and within a radius of one hundred *bracci fiorentini* (a *braccio fiorentino* = 58.4 cm).

Plaque dated 26 January 1701, at 8, Piazza Tasso, prohibiting all games and rowdiness.

Plaque dated 1742 in Piazza Giglio, prohibiting all ballgames.

VEDUTA DELLA PIAZZA DI S.ta CROCE DELLA CITTA DI FIRENZE NEL ATTO DI PRINCIPIARE IL GIOCO DEL CALCIO A.o 1688

FLORENTINE FOOTBALL

Dating back to the Renaissance, the historic game of "Florentine football" is sometimes considered the ancestor of the modern-day version. However, the rules and the physical contact in the game make it more similar to rugby than to football.

The players in the Renaissance came from the four historic districts into which Florence was divided: Santo Spirito (white), Santa Maria Novella (red), San Giovanni (green) and Santa Croce (blue). Usually scions of the local nobility, the players had to be aged between 18 and 45; the rather magnificent strip or liveries they wore would lead to this game also being known as calcio in costume and calcio in livrea. There were 27 players on each side and the fifty-minute games were played on a field covered with sand. The aim was to get the ball into the opposing team's net. Whilst the rules were not entirely "anything goes", the game was quite violent and it was not unusual for a match to end in a free-for-all. The winning team received a Chianina heifer (a prized breed of cattle from Val di Chiana). A number of matches would become famous. In 1491 and 1605, for example, the game was actually played on the frozen surface of the Arno. Then there was the match of 1530, which took place while the city was under siege by Papal forces, showing its defiance by not altering its Carnival plans in spite of the shortage of food. The besieging forces were thus able to watch the match from the hills above the city, though far from entering into the spirit of the thing they actually fired a cannonball during the match... to which the Florentines responded with loud booing. In 1575 the Florentine merchants in Lyon organised a match in that city – an event that was commemorated during the 1998 French World Cup by a July match between Florence and Lyon. And, finally, there is the 1766 match played in Livorno. One of the spectators was the English consul, and it is said that what he saw resulted in the development of the modern game of football in his home country.

Famous players of Florentine football included various members of the Medici family and even three popes: Clement VII, Leo XI and Urban VIII (the latter was actually born at 5, Piazza Santa Croce).

The game went into decline in the 17th century, and the last known match in pre-modern Florence was played in 1739. Then in 1930, the 400th anniversary of the above-mentioned siege of the city was marked by a resumption of the tradition. Today there is an annual tournament in the month of June that involves all four historic districts, with two eliminating matches and a final, all played before a crowd of 100,000 spectators on a sand-covered Piazza Santa Croce. Unfortunately, on 11 June 2006, the first match of the tournament – between the Whites of Santa Spirito and the Blues of Santa Croce – degenerated into a brawl and had to be interrupted. As a result, the tournaments of 2006 and 2007 were cancelled.

MERIDIAN IN FLORENCE'S ISTITUTO ㉕

1, Piazza Dei Giudici
- Tel. : 055 226 53 11
- Call service: 055 29 34 93
- E-mail : info@imss.fi.it
- www.imss.firenze.it
- Opening hours: 1 June to 30 September: Monday, Wednesday, Thursday and Friday 9.30-17.00; Tuesday and Saturday 9.30-13.00. Closed Sunday, 2 June, 24 June and 15 August. 1 October to 31 May: Monday, Wednesday, Thursday and Friday 9.30-17.00; Tuesday 9.30-13.00. Second Sunday of the month 10.00-13.00. Closed on other Sundays, as well as 1 November, 8, 25 and 26 December, 1 and 6 January, Easter and Easter Monday, 25 April and 1 May.
Admission: 7.50 €, reduced: 4 €.

" *Commemorating Florentine science*

The superb meridian that adorns the forecourt of the History of Science Museum was unveiled in 2008 and celebrates the combination of tradition (of which the museum is the custodian) and modernity.

The signs of the zodiac in glass are laid out in the ground along a calibrated copper standard that runs for fifteen meters from the Arno parapet (where the summer solstice is marked) to the museum entrance (where the winter solstice is marked) As well as functioning as a calendar, the instrument can also function as a solar clock, thanks to the calibrations in the metal. The gnomon, in fact, stands 6.19 metres high and consists of a double blade of bronze which rises from a water basin bordered with a wind rose.

Another traditional feature is the inclusion of a zoomorphic sub-meridian; the gnomon, in the form of a lizard's tail, indicates the exact moment when the sun is at its highest point. At night, the entire instrument is lit up, making it a feature of the city's urban landscape.

The museum itself houses both a permanent collection and temporary exhibitions on specific themes. The former include some unique pieces: sundials, astrolabes, solar clocks, nocturnal clocks, compasses, armillary spheres, and several of Galileo's original instruments (including his famous first spyglass). The library and research centre underline this institution's importance as a custodian of Florence's past as a centre of scientific enquiry.

OUTSIDE FLORENCE

"RIDOTTA INVALIDA
PREFERÍ LA MORTE"
IN MEMORIA
DELLA
BISTECCA
ALLA FIORENTINA
SCOMPARSA PREMATURAMENTE
IL 31 MARZO 2001

LE MIE PREGHIERE ALFIN FURONO ACCOLTE
TORNA LA FIORENTINA E BEN CI AZZECCA
INVALIDA MORÍ
VISSE DUE VOLTE
E INFATTI IL NOME SUO OGGI É:

BISTECCA!

ALBERTO SEVERI PER DARIO CECCHINI IL 21 GENNAIO 2006

THE CECCHINI BUTCHER'S SHOP

❶

11, Via XX Luglio. 50022 Panzano in Chianti (FI)
- Tel: 055 85 20 20
- E-mail: macelleriacecchini@tin.it
- Closed on Wednesday.
- "Solo ciccia" menu (meat only): 30 €
- Opening hours: three sittings, at 13.00, 19.00 and 21.00

*He who eats
La Fiorentina
is fearless*

When, on 1 April 2001, the sale of beef on the bone was forbidden because of bovine spongiform encephalopathy (BSE, or mad-cow disease), Dario Cecchini set up a funeral plaque in front of his butcher's shop. It read: "Reduced to infirmity, we prefer death. In memory of the Fiorentina steak, whose premature demise occurred on 31 March 2001." However, in October 2005 the ban was lifted and the T-bone steak was back.

Dario Cecchini has launched a very original lunch and dinner menu of solo ciccia [meat only], which is served at a single table: five portions of meat of your choice, two vegetables, bread, wine and coffee – all for 30?. There is one sitting at lunch (13.00) and two in the evening (19.00 and 21.00). Another original feature: you can bring your own wine. But you would be missing out on something if you did not trust Dario to choose for you (his shop is situated right in the heart of Chianti country).

Apart from the food, a visit here is to be recommended for the atmosphere, the hospitality, and the banter. Dario, after all, is someone whose calling-card reads: "He who eats La Fiorentina is fearless".

DARIO CECCHINI'S RECIPE FOR BISTECCA PANZANESE

The bistecca Panzanese is the massive centre cut from a leg of choice Cecchini beef. Vacuum-packed and stored in a refrigerator, it will keep for a month. Here are the rules to follow in order to get the best out of it:
- Remove from the fridge some 10-12 hours before cooking.
- Cook on red-hot embers or a flat griddle: 5 minutes per side, and 15 minutes "upright" on one side.
- Do not use any metal implements to turn it; only a wooden spatula or your hands.
- Serve, already cut, on a wooden chopping-board.

True gourmets eat a Panzanese steak without adding any sauce, in order to enjoy the flavour to the full. The only acceptable additives are a little extra-virgin olive oil and a pinch of profumo Chianti (a herb and salt mix prepared at the Cecchini Butcher's).

This is not only food, it is a real emotion. A way of truly biting into life! Wash down with copious glasses of red wine... Chianti classico, of course.

Note that this recipe is very similar to that for the traditional Fiorentina.

THE PRISONS OF PALAZZO PRETORIO ❷

Via Boccaccio
50052 Certaldo (FI)
• Tel: 0571 66 12 19
• Opening hours: in summer, daily 10.00-19.00; in winter, daily (except Monday) 10.00-16.30.
• Admission: 3 €, reduced: 1.50 €.

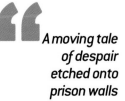

A moving tale of despair etched onto prison walls

Located near the top of the main street in the elegant old town of Certaldo, Palazzo Pretorio contains courtrooms, torture rooms, and cells – each of which has fascinating details. In the audience chamber, the wall bears the magistrate's motto: "Listen to the opposing side…without believing too much."

To the side of this room, a large holding cell has walls covered with graffiti. The words reach up to the vaulted ceiling; it is even said that the prisoners formed human pyramids so that one of their number could get up to use whatever blank space was left. The signatures on the walls include those of "Giambadia Neri, Castelfiorentino" and "Giambattista Perazini 1555." A regular of this prison, Giambadia was something of an artist. One finds mention of him in another inscription made using candle soot. "Oh, how badly things are going for you, my friend. When you have set foot inside, it no longer depends on you when you leave. Giambadia knows this, and that is why he is telling you."

The prison for male convicts is particularly appalling, with narrow windowless cells that can only be reached by crawling through a low and very narrow tunnel. One of the three extant cells can still be visited. On the walls, the graffiti from the period gives us some idea of how atrocious a prisoner's life must have been. Look, for example, at the sun scratched into the wall, each ray representing a day that the prisoner has been shut away in this dungeon. The torture chamber was linked directly with the cells, making it possible to extract confessions more efficiently.

SIGHTS NEARBY:

THE CUPOLA OF THE SEMIFONTE CHAPEL
Chapel of San Michele Arcangelo
Semifonte
50021 Barberino Val d'Elsa (FI)
Opening hours: Sunday 15.30-19.30.
Free admission
Directions: Take the road from Barberino to Certaldo. The chapel is 1km beyond the village of Petrognano.

The chapel of San Michele Arcangelo at Barberino Val d'Elsa is remarkable in that its cupola is a perfect model (scale 1:8) of the dome of Florence Cathedral. The twelfth century was a period of economic boom for the town of Semifonte, due largely to the settlement's location on the Via Francigena. Enclosed by more than three kilometres of walls, the town had a population of some 300 families, each engaged in various business activities. Viewing this success with a jaundiced eye, the Florentines attempted to take the town a number of times, and finally succeeded after a long, hard siege. Their animus was such that they razed the place to the ground, forbidding future reconstruction. It was not until 1594 that anything would be built here: a chapel for which Giovan Battista di Neri Capponi had obtained permission from the Grande Duke, Ferdinando I. Consecrated in 1597, the chapel and its replica cupola had a double function: acknowledging Florentine dominion, it was also a reminder that it was the Florentines who had destroyed Semifonte.

THE SACRO MONTE OF SAN VIVALDO

❹

Convent of San Vivaldo
San Vivaldo
50050 Montaione (FI)

*An amazing
reconstruction of
Christ's Passion*

Created on the site where Vivaldo de San Gimignano* died, the San Valdo Sacro Monte recreates various places associated with the life and final Passion of Christ. The twenty or so extant chapels (in the 16th century there were a total of 34) are adorned with sculpted reliefs and frescoes that depict such scenes as the Flight into Egypt and "Noli Me Tangere" ("Do Not Touch Me," the words used by the risen Christ to Mary Magdalene). There is also a House of Herod, a House of Caiaphas the High Priest and a House of St. Anne (the Virgin's mother). The entire place has a very special atmosphere – particularly during periods of good weather, when masses and religious services are held here.

The idea for such "holy mounts" dates back to the 15th/16th century. They were created so that the faithful could, without exposing themselves to all of the hazards of a journey to the Holy Land, still make a pilgrimage that evoked the scenes of Christ's Passion. The Franciscan Friars Minor chose three locations for these "New Jerusalems:" Varallo in Lombardy, Montaione in Tuscany and Braga in Portugal.

After the Council of Trent, they also became an increasingly effective way of combating the influence of the Protestant Reform. The model most frequently followed was that of the Varallo Sacro Monte, which had been created in about 1480. Throughout the 16th and 17th centuries, and even up to the middle of the 18th, more sacri monti were created throughout Italy – for example at Crea,

Orta, Varese, Oropa, Ossuccio, Ghiffa, Domodossdola and Valperga – dedicated not only to the life of Christ but also to the Virgin, the Holy Trinity, the Rosary, and the lives of the saints. Although at the beginning they followed similar basic rules, as the years went on, each would develop its own artistic and architectural characteristics.

* Vivaldo de San Gimignano (c.1250-1320). Now beatified, Vivaldo de San Gimignano was a hermit who lived in the hollowed trunk of a chestnut tree, on the site of which it is said that the monastery dedicated to his name was later built. The truth is that there was already a church here, dedicated to an earlier Vivaldo.

CONSTELLATIONS OF THE CATHEDRAL OF SANTA ⑤ MARIA ASSUNTA E SAN GENESIO

Prato del Duomo
56027 San Miniato (PI)

> *Ursa Major, Ursa Minor, and the Pole Star on a cathedral façade*

The brick façade of the cathedral of San Miniato is adorned with 32 majolica bowls of unknown origin (perhaps from Moorish Spain, perhaps from North Africa). They are, curiously enough, laid out to recreate the two constellations of Ursa Major and Ursa Minor. At the top is a white and green star that represents the Pole Star. The originals of these majolica bowls are now in the Episcopal Palace.

The ornamentation was installed at the behest of Emperor Fredrick II, who was passionately interested in astronomy and astrology. He was also responsible for the construction of the nearby fortress and the tower that bears his name; destroyed by the Germans in 1944, it was rebuilt in 1958.

The constellations are a symbolic representation of the heaven in which the earthly journey of the Christian should culminate. Similarly, the Pole Star, in the north, is the direction towards which the compass needle points, and symbolically associated with the first gesture of the Sign of the Cross, upwards, towards God the Father.

FREDERIC II

Fredrick II (1194-1250) was born on a special podium raised in the main square of Jesi (near Ancona); the bed on which his mother gave birth was closely guarded so that no one could claim the child was a changeling and therefore contest his right to the crown. Orphaned when very young, Frederick was already King of Sicily when he was crowned Holy Roman Emperor in 1220. This coronation came after a series of historic turnarounds, the most spectacular of which was the defeat of his rival, Otto IV, at the battle of Bouvines (France) in 1214. Various features of the emperor's biography – his relations with various popes, the crusade he undertook, his amazing number of wives and lovers (he had a veritable harem), and the number of children he sired – all these make him into a character who seems somehow to symbolise the time in which he lived, a period of both enlightenment and trepidation. Author of a manual on falconry and a champion of what might be considered modern medicine, Frederick was a skilful politician who spoke nine languages. Throughout his life he would avoid staying in Florence (then called Florentia) because he had been told that he would die in a city whose name contained the word 'flower' (fiore in Italian). However, he met his death at a place whose name he did not know: Castel Fiorentino. There are numerous traces of Frederick II in Italy, most notably the Castel del Monte which he had built at Andria in Puglia – this now appears on the 1 eurocent coin.

STATUE OF THE VIRGIN IN THE CLOISTER OF ❻
THE COLLEGIATE CHURCH OF SANT'ANDREA

Museum of the Collegiate Church of Sant'Andrea
3, Piazzetta della Propositura
50053 Empoli (FI)
• Tel: 0571 76284
• E-mail: cultura@comune.empoli.fi.it
• Opening hours: 9.00-12.00 and 16.00-19.00. Closed Monday.
• Admission: 3 €, reduced: 1.5 €.

> *A Catholic sculpture paid for by a ghetto Jew...*

The glazed terracotta statue of the Virgin and Child in the cloister of the Collegiate Church of Sant'Andrea is by the Della Robbia school. Curiously enough, it was paid for by a Jewish resident of the town's ghetto.

In 1518, whilst the Corpus Christi procession was passing by his house, the banker Zaccaria d'Isacco could not resist – perhaps because of the tension caused by the recent imposed baptism of a Jewish infant – making derogatory comments when the baldaquin with the monstrance (a receptacle for the Host) came to a halt beneath his windows. Tried in Florence – to avoid public indignation resulting in violence – the banker was sentenced to pay for a statue of the Virgin and Child. Originally set into the façade of the Palazzo Pretorio, the statue was moved to its present location during the period of Napoleonic rule: it was considered to be too crude a reminder of religious intolerance. The circumstances which resulted in the removal of the infant's head are unknown.

« Photograph: Museo della Collegiata di Sant'Andrea »

SIGHTS NEARBY:
WOODEN WINGS OF A FLYING ASS

7

Cloister Museum of the Collegiate Church of Sant'Andrea
3, Piazzetta della Propositura

In the same cloister as the statue of the Virgin (see above) is a curious pair of wood wings (complete with pulleys) suspended from the ceiling. These were the wings for the ass which "flew" each year from the top of the bell tower down to Piazza Farinata degli Uberti (also known as Piazza dei Leoni) during the evening which ended the Corpus Domini celebrations.

The tradition dated back to 1397, when the forces of the city of Empoli took the castle of San Miniato, which had been considered impregnable. The besieging forces had hit upon the ruse of strapping lamps to a thousand goats which they then drove up towards the castle: believing that they were massively outnumbered, the defenders surrendered and opened their gates to avoid being put to the sword. The Captain of the castle, a certain Silvera, had previously boasted that he would surrender when asses could fly – and thus the tradition of the "flying ass" was a mocking reference to his words. The poor animal concerned was strapped into a winged harness (as you can see at the museum) which ran on two pulleys along a rope. From the top of the bell tower, the creature was then released to travel the length of the cable and smash against one of the columns in the piazza. The custom was finally banned in 1860 – not only because of its cruelty but also because it mocked Empoli's ancient rival of San Miniato. In 1981 an attempt was made to revive the custom using a model of an ass; but due to its cost, this revival lasted only a few years.

THE GALLENO SECTION OF THE VIA FRANCIGENA

8

Via della Chiesa Galleno
50054 Fucecchio (FI)
• Directions: Having reached the village of Galleno, which lies between Altopascio and Fucecchio, take Via della Chiesa and then leave your car in the car park in front of the church. The section of the old Via Francigena begins right there.

All roads lead to Rome

T he Galleno section of the old *Via Francigena* is a pleasant stretch of stone paving in the midst of a bucolic landscape. A wooden bridge over the small Rio Torbo soon brings you to the now-abandoned hostelry of I Greppi, which once upon a time had a very bad reputation: it was there that high-waymen often identified those whom they would subsequently offer the choice of "your money or your life." From here, the stone paving runs on towards the more modern world, meeting the tarmac road after 1.2 km.

This section of ancient road is also marked by a stele set up in 2006 when 70 former Swiss Guards retraced the route followed by the 150 original Swiss Guards who had been summoned to Rome in 1505 by Pope Julius II. Each stele is placed by a tree (see Altopascio, page 211).

THE VIA FRANCIGENA

Extending a total of 1,700 km, the old Via Francigena was the pilgrimage route from Rome to Canterbury. Its traditional path is that described by Sigeric, Archbishop of Canterbury and Primate of the Church in England, who went to Rome in 990 to meet Pope John XV.

Along with the roads to Santiago de Compostela and the route to Jerusalem, this was one of the three great pilgrimage roads of the Middle Ages. The

entire route is still intact, and can be followed from one end to the other, either on foot or by bicycle. The 79 different stages are known to us from an original text now in the British Library. The name obviously reflects that this was once the "road of the Franks." However, those who travelled along it towards Rome were also known roumieux in French – the origin of the Italian name Romeo.

PASSION CROSS IN THE MONASTERY OF SANTA MARIA A RIPA ❾

36, Via Porta di Borgo
51016 Montecatini Alto (PT)
• Tel: 0572 91 15 88
Park in the small area in front of the monastery. The Cross is to one side of the steps that lead to the church.

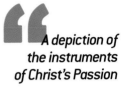

A depiction of the instruments of Christ's Passion

This fine example of a Passion Cross at Santa Maria a Ripa is noteworthy not only for its size but also for its detailed reproductions of the implements used by Christ's tormenters (most of these are in wood).

From the top to the bottom of the Cross, one finds a total of thirty or so such objects: the panel reading 'INRI' [Jesus of Nazareth, King of the Jews], the Crown of Thorns, the hand symbolising that washed by Pontius Pilate, the Vernicle bearing the image of Christ's face (not to be confused with the Holy Shroud, see below), the sword with which Peter cut off the ear of Malchus, the lantern by whose light Malchus recognised Jesus in the Garden of Olives, the cup in which Christ's blood was collected (this would become the Holy Grail) the tunic for which the Roman soldiers cast dice (along with the dice immediately below), and the veil of the maidservant Ancilla. Right at the base of the Cross is a skull that recalls the place of Christ's crucifixion, Mount Golgotha (gulgota in Aramaic means "skull").

On the left arm of the Cross are: the rope used to heave it into place, the spear which pierced Christ's side, the pitcher containing the vinegar he was given to drink, the pincers used to draw out the nails, and the ladder used to bring his body down after the crucifixion. Located on the right arm are the column to which Christ was bound during the flagellation, the cockerel which crowed three times, the hammer which drove in the nails, the long rod with the sponge soaked in vinegar, and the whip with flails. The three nails themselves are in the places where they held Christ's hands and feet.

This already impressive list of items also includes the purse with the thirty pieces of silver which Judas accepted to betray Christ, the heart symbolising Christ's love for humankind, and the Sun recalling that there was an eclipse of three hours at Christ's death.

THE VERNICLE

According to the apocryphal gospels (particularly that of Nicodemus), as Christ was bearing his Cross to Golgotha a woman drew off her veil to wipe his brow. The image of Christ's face would remain imprinted on the material and miraculously survive over the centuries. Later, the name of this woman would be given as Veronica, from the Latin vero (true) and the Greek icon (image), with the veil itself becoming known in English as the Vernicle. Various churches (in Rome, Milan or Jaén in Spain) claim to possess the original Vernicle. The one now displayed in St. Peter's in Rome was first described in 1137.

ENIGMATIC HEADS ON BUILDINGS IN PISTOIA 🔟

- Palazzo Communale, Piazza del Duomo
- Church of Sant'Andrea, Via Sant'Andrea
- Corner of Via Sant'Andrea and Via de'Rossi
- Via Borgostrada (first wall on the left upon leaving Piazza dello Spirito Santo)

Heads up...

When visiting Pistoia, you would do well to glance upwards now and again: numerous walls and buildings are adorned with sculpted heads whose meaning is not always clear.

The most spectacular – and best known – of these heads is to be found on the façade of the Palazzo Communale. It is surmounted by an arm brandishing a weapon; the sharp-eyed will also make out a bunch of keys hanging around the arm itself. Some have claimed that the head depicts King Musetto of Majorca, who was defeated by the Pistoia-born Grandone de' Ghisilieri when the Pisan fleet conquered the Balearic Islands in 1115. However, a more likely suspect would be Filippo Tedici, who treacherously seized power in 1325 with the backing of the town of Lucca. Having been overthrown and driven out of Pistoia, he would later try to incite a popular uprising against the occupying forces of Guelph-controlled Florence. But recognised by some peasants at the Castruccio bridge which crossed the river Lima near Popiglio (see Castruccio Castracani in the section on Lucca, page 185), Tedici was killed and his head was then borne in triumph to Pistoia on a pike. The city's Council of Elders would decide that marble effigies of the traitor should be carved and placed at various points in Pistoia (ruling of 7 September 1336) as a warning to other traitors.

As for the keys, they open the doors to the city gaols. They were added in 1399, when those still languishing in prison as a result of intestine strife were finally released thanks to the intercession of the bishop, Andrea Franchi, and the payment of a ransom collected during a day of penitence.

Effigies of the head of Filippo Tedici are to be found in three other places: at the corner of Via Sant'Andrea and Via de' Rossi, on a column to the right of the main doorway to the church of Sant'Andrea and at the beginning of Via Borgostrada as it leads out of Piazza dello Spirito Santo. The face embedded in the Sant'Andrea column in fact looks more porcine than human. It is said that the city gravediggers used to show their contempt for the traitor by extinguishing their torches against the effigy.

THE DEATH OF GERMANICUS
BY NICOLAS POUSSIN
(ORIGINAL PAINTING IN THE MINNEAPOLIS INSTITUTE OF ARTS, USA)

⑪

Corner Room C
Museo Clemente Rospigliosi
9, Via Ripa del Sale
• Tel: 0573 28 740
• Opening hours: Tuesday to Saturday 10.00-13.00 and 18.00-19.00.

> *When Poussin copied his own paintings...*

Connoisseurs visiting the Museo Rospigliosi in Pistoia will undoubtedly come to a halt before the painting entitled The Death of Germanicus. An extremely faithful copy of the original work by Nicolas Poussin, this is remarkable in that it was painted by Poussin himself.

Seeking to study Italian painting that he admired so much, Poussin set out for Rome, where he hoped to perfect his own art. However, health problems meant that his first two attempts to get there were unsuccessful. During his first journey, he intended to stop in Florence, but due to sickness he had to spend some time convalescing in Pistoia, where he lodged with the Puccini family. To thank his hosts, he painted this copy of *The Death of Germanicus*, a work he had previously carried out for Cardinal Barberini.

As Félibien notes, Poussin "preferred to be the copyist of his own works, rather than entrusting the task to someone else." The original painting would remain in the Barberini collection until 1958, when it was acquired by the Minneapolis Institute of Arts.

SIGHTS NEARBY:

"BE PATIENT" STREET

⑫

This curious street name – Via Abbi Pazienza (be patient) – can be seen on the wall to the left of number 1 of the road which starts by the church of Sant'Andrea: above a small drinking fountain is a stone plaque on which the (scarcely legible) words "Abi pacenzia" seem to emerge from a man's mouth.

The most plausible explanation dates back to the Middle Ages, a period when it was not unusual for members of rival clans to ambush each other in the street, sometimes with fatal consequences. The story goes that one night a man crouching within the alcove of the drinking-fountain awaited his enemy with murderous intent. Seeing a shadow emerge from the darkness, he hurled himself upon the figure, dagger at the ready. However, he stopped the blow just in time when he realised that he had been about to strike dead not his rival but a close friend. After this lucky escape, the friend then slipped off into the night, encouraging the would-be assassin to "be patient."

MYSTIC MARRIAGE OF THE BISHOP AND THE ABBESS

Up to the middle of the 16th century, the appointment of a new bishop in Pistoia was marked by the very unusual ceremony of a "mystic marriage." The future bishop passed the night before his investiture outside the city, on the road from Pistoia to Lucca. Garbed in his ceremonial vestments, he rode into the town the next day on a white horse, accompanied by various notables; from the gate on the Pistoia-Lucca road, he then processed to the church of the convent of San Pietro. Here, a ceremony of "marriage" between the bishop and the abbess of the convent was performed. After an exchange of rings, the two knelt beside a richly adorned bed set up in the centre of the church. The ceremony binding together the bishop and the main female figure of authority in Pistoia was seen as marking the union of civil and religious power.

One can well imagine the determination with which the Counter Reformation set about abolishing the sexual symbolism of the bed and the exchange of rings... and eventually the entire ceremony itself. However, the event did survive in the work of a Danish artist, Kristian Zahrtmann, an indefatigable explorer of all things Italian. When he heard of this curious – but by then extinct – custom, Zahrtmann made it the subject of a spectacular work, his *The Mystic Marriage of Pistoia (The marriage between the Bishop and Abbess of Pistoia celebrated before the church of san Pietro in the year 1500)*. Measuring 1.23 metre by 1.46, the work was exhibited for the first time in Copenhagen in 1894; it is now to be found in the Museum of the Island of Bornholm in Denmark. A fascinating book entitled *Kristian Zahrtmann e il Matrimonio Mistico di Pistoia* is on sale for 18 euros at the Pistoia city museum (unfortunately it is only available in Italian). Along with numerous illustrations of Zahrtmann's work, the book contains a fine reproduction of the painting.

PISTOIA MUSEUM OF SURGICAL IMPLEMENTS ⑬

Ospedale del Ceppo
1, Piazza Giovanni XXIII
51100 Pistoia (PT)
• Free admission, but visits by appointment only – phone: 0573 35 20 40

An extraordinary anatomy theatre

Still a functioning hospital, the Ospedale del Ceppo contains a Museum of Surgical Implements that is a veritable gem. The high point of the visit is the extraordinary 17th century anatomy theatre. This has recently been restored, complete with original furnishings which give one a vivid idea of what the place must have once been like. The anteroom is dominated by a simple white marble slab, where the cadaver was laid out before the lesson began. A curious hinged contraption in wood made it possible to hold the limbs in place ready for study. In the second room are the narrow benches of the amphitheatre. The place could seat around forty students, all gazing down at the second marble slab where the anatomical dissection actually took place. The room's walls are decorated with painted grotesques that are strangely out of keeping with the purpose of the theatre itself.

The museum proper begins with a room containing exhibits of dozens of surgical implements dating from the 18th and 19th century. Used by obstetricians, urologists, and orthopaedists, some of these tools were manufactured outside Italy (in France and England) but most were produced in Pistoia itself, a city still renowned for its skill in this field. The exhibits include a pair of the famous forceps invented at the beginning of the eighteenth century by Peter Chamberlen, a Frenchman with an Anglicised name. In fact, he long kept the design of a secret so as to enjoy a very profitable exclusivity over his invention… And don't miss the amazing obstetric "machine," which enabled students to perform simulated deliveries. Damaged during the bombing raids of the Second World War, this contraption has unfortunately lost the accessories that went with it: a false placenta made out of fabric, a toy baby, and a dead foetus.

> The hospital owes its curious name (*del ceppo* means "of the stump") to that fact that the stump of a chestnut tree was used to collect donations towards the cost of the original building.

THE SCAPEL: A PISTOIAN INVENTION

Curiously enough, the Italian word for scalpel (*bisturi*) comes from the French term *bistouri*, which itself is derived from the word *Pistorese* ("from Pistoia:" the city was renowned for its production of sharp-bladed instruments). A very interesting example of how terms move backwards and forwards between different languages.

SIGHTS NEARBY:

CENTRO ISTRUZIONE E CULTURA – CAFFÉ LA CIVETTA ⑭

19, Via Corrado da Montemagro
51039 Quarrata (PT)
Opening hours: 6.30-20.00. Closed on Sunday

Only recently turned into a café, this municipal-owned building has a very unusual façade designed by the architect Stefano Mirti. Certified as an architect in Turin and Tokyo, Mirti now divides his time Italy and the Far East.

THE MALAPARTE MUSEUM ⑮

Monte le Coste (531 m). Cerreto. 59100 Prato (PO)

Curzio Malaparte, real name Kurt-Erich Suckert, was born on 9 June 1898 in Prato. The son of an Italian mother and German father, he would when 17 years old enlist to fight with the Italian army in France. During the Second World War he initially fought for the Fascists but was then purged from Mussolini's political party. Joining the camp of the Allies, Malaparte subsequently became one of most admired war correspondents reporting on the conflict, his articles being read worldwide. His two novels *Kaputt* and La Pelle would then make him a rich and famous author. His last book was *Maledetti Toscani* (damned Tuscans). A masterpiece that offers subjective and ironic analysis of his adopted homeland, the work is rich in savage yet tongue-in-cheek humour. In another demonstration of his ironic sense of humour, on the very eve of his death, Malaparte would become a member of the Italian Communist Party... simply to be sure that the Party would have one less member the following day!

His last wishes are graven in stone: "I would like my tomb to be up there, at the top of Monte Spazzavento, in order to raise my head every now and again and spit into the cold Tramontane wind." However, his actual tomb is on Monte le

Coste, not far from Prato; the name Spazzavento (wind-blown) was another of the author's inventions.

His sober funeral monument has a wall with a single opening and a single stone sarcophagus. Not far way stands a stone on which these words are engraved: 'I am from Prato. I am proud of being from Prato. And I would rather never have been born than not to have been born in Prato'.

Directions: It is a good two hours' walk to and from the Malaparte Mausoleum, involving a change in altitude of over 200 metres. You must have good walking shoes for the trip. From the Prato ring road (*circonvallazione*), turn left towards Fegline. Just after the village, turn right on the narrow road to Cerreto. At the end of this road, after the small village, one can see the beginning of the footpath, marked by a rusty signpost that clearly dates from the erection of the mausoleum in 1961 (some four years after Malaparte's death). After a good uphill stretch, the path crosses route no. 10, onto which you should then turn right and continue up to the summit; the path is indicated by red-and-white and blue-and-white markers.

MUSEUM OF VINTAGE AMBULANCES (AND HEARSES)

16

32, Piazza Leonardo da Vinci, 59013 Montemurlo (PO)
• Tel: 339 46 23 62? • Visits by appointment only
• For opening hours (yet to be established) see: www.volontari.org

> *Vintage ambulances, with a friar as your guide*

Set up by the Confraternity of Montemurlo – itself a subsidiary branch of the *Venerabile Arciconfraternità della Misericordia di Prato* (see below) - this ambulance museum is an astonishing place. Located within the industrial zone of Montemurlo, it was opened in October 2006 and has more than 50 ambulances and 10 hearses, all in perfect condition. The earliest exhibits date back to when the sick were carried on foot by stretcher bearers. Thereafter are examples of cars adapted by local body shops to serve as ambulances ; this was in the days before such vehicles were purpose-built. Each ambulance is accompanied by the relevant technical details. But what brings this museum to life is the commentary provided by the friar from the confraternity 'brother' who accompanies you and knows anecdotes relating to each ambulance.

The 1943 Willys MB Jeep, for example, arrived in Italy with American troops during the Second World War. After the war it was bought by Father Aldo Fazzini, parish priest of Schignano, and was converted into an ambulance by a body shop in Prato. It would perform sterling service right up to the day that the group bought it for the museum and then restored it before putting it on display. When Father Fazzini came to visit the museum and saw the old ambulance, his eyes lit up. "That's her!" he said, without further comment.

CONFRATERNITA' DELLA MISERICORDIA

These confraternities were founded in the 13th century to assist pilgrims and provide them with lodging. Catholic in origin, they would adapt over the centuries to met the needs of changing events (epidemics, famine, war) and societies, concerning themselves not only with the transport of the sick and wounded but also with the collectionof those who died penniless in the street and even with the collection of funds to provide needy young women with dowries. The brothersof the confraternity wore a long ankle-length robe, which during the plague of 1630 became black in colour (in order to hide the stains left by the discharge from purulent sores). They also wore a hood with two eyeholes, which was intended to guarantee that their charitable work remained anonymous. Their robes, complete with a rope that serves as a belt, have remained unchanged to the present day, when they are only worn for formal processions.

Today, the various Confraternità della Misericordia are the backbone of Italy's ambulance services.

THE HANDPRINT IN PRATO CATHEDRAL

Piazza del Duomo
59100 Prato (PO)

The bloody trace of the hand that wished to steal the holy relic of the Virgin's girdle...

To the upper left of the second door in the south wall of the cathedral – that nearest the bell tower – is a curious age-old mark. Consisting of the print of a thumb and four fingers, it is said to belong to a thief who tried to steal the famous and precious relic of the Virgin's Girdle (see below). According to the story, around 1141 a certain Michele dei Dagomari, a resident of Prato, married the daughter of a priest in Jerusalem, a certain Maria, who brought this girdle as her dowry. After various vicissitudes, the man would donate the relic to the city in 1175. In 1312, Giovanni di Landetto, a canon living in Pistoia, managed to lay his hands on it. But on his way back home, he got lost in the fog and unwittingly walked in a circle back to one the Prato town gates. There, he shouted: "Open up, I have the Holy Girdle from Prato!" Captured, he had his right hand amputated and was then led off to be burnt at the stake. The angry crowd seized his severed hand and hurled it against the cathedral. It is said to have struck the wall at the above-mentioned place, leaving a bloody hand.

THE HOLY GIRDLE – THE DORMITION AND ASSUMPTION OF THE VIRGIN

The relic of the Holy Girdle of the Virgin is preserved in a chapel to which it gives its name.

The story associated with this relic dates back to St. Thomas, and is itself linked with the apocryphal episode of the Dormition of the Virgin (which figures primarily in the Gospel of St. John the Theologian). According to this tradition, the Virgin did not actually die but rather "fell asleep." She rendered her soul to God in the presence of all the other Apostles with the exception of St. Thomas. He arrived late and, refusing to believe in her Assumption, opened her tomb, where he found nothing but lilies and roses. Thomas then raised his head heavenwards, where he saw the Virgin in glory. Untying her girdle, she handed it to him as a gift, and as proof that she had ascended to Heaven "in body and soul." The tradition of the Dormition and Assumption did not become Church dogma until 1 November 1950 – when a five-year-old boy, Gilles Bouhours, is said to have passed on to Pope Pius XII a message he received from the Virgin, who appeared to him in visions. "The Holy Virgin is not dead," the boy told him. "she ascended to Heaven both body and soul." Note that there are three other relics of the Holy Girdle: at Puy-Notre-Dame in France, at Homs in Syria and at Istanbul in Turkey. St. Isidor, too, is said to have received the Virgin's girdle as proof of her Assumption into Heaven.

ASSUMPTION AND ASCENSION

The Ascension refers to Christ's ascension to Heaven, while the Assumption refers to the raising of the Virgin. The latter term indicates a passive process: the body of the Virgin did not raise itself heavenward.

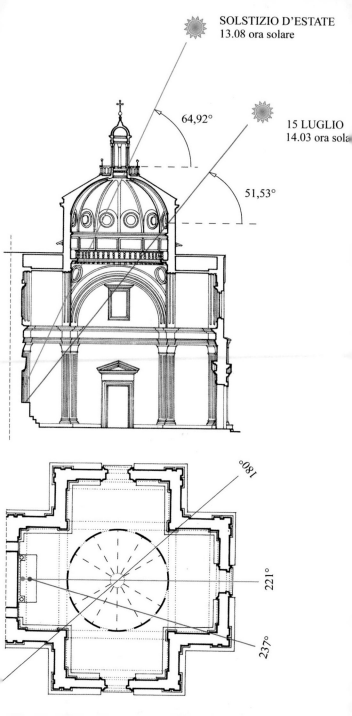

SOLSTIZIO D'ESTATE
13.08 ora solare

15 LUGLIO
14.03 ora solare

64,92°

51,53°

180°

221°

237°

BASILICA OF SANTA MARIA DELLE CARCERI ⓲

Piazza Santa Maria delle Carceri
59100 Prato (PO)

When science works miracles...

Tradition has it that on 6 July 1484 a child saw the image of the Virgin and Child painted on the walls of the Prato prison begin to move. After the phenomenon was repeated a number of times, the basilica of Santa Maria delle Carceri ("of prisons") was built on the site. The architect Giuliano da Sangallo began work in 1485, creating a church in the form of a Greek cross. The alignment of the building was very carefully calculated so that on the anniversary of the miracle (the 15th of July according to the Gregorian calendar adopted in 1582), a ray of sunlight would fall directly onto the centre of the high altar at the precise hour of 15.19 (14.03 solar time). Furthermore, the axis of the building was so calculated that on the day of the summer solstice (21 June) the azimuth of the sun would correspond with the structure's angle of alignment (221°) and a ray of light falling down through the cupola would illuminate the revered image of the Virgin....

The intention was not so much to create belief in a new miracle as to preserve the original miracle of 1484 by reproducing it each year. The sanctuary has continued to be a place of devotion and still attracts large numbers of the faithful on these two special days.

SIGHTS NEARBY:

ITALY'S LARGEST METEOR ⓳

Museum of Planetary Sciences
20/H, Via Galcianese
Tel: 0574 44 771.
Email: info@mspo.it. www.mspo.it

Opening hours: from September to May, Tuesday to Sunday 8.30-13.30 and 15.00-17.00; June to August, Tuesday to Friday 9.00-13.00 and 17.00-23.00, Saturday and Sunday 9.00-13.00 and 16.00-20.00.

Admission: 5 €, reduced: 2.50 €.

Opened in March 2005, the new Museum of Planetary Sciences in Prato contains various amazing meteorites, including the largest one in Italy. Known as the Nantan Meteorite, it weighs 272kg – and one is even allowed to touch it! It is a rare example of a ferrous meteorite and fell near the Chinese village of Nantan in 1516, being discovered there by local peasants in 1958. Its composition is 92% iron and 7% nickel.

Meteorites are in fact classified according to the weight they have while still in space, before falling into the Earth's atmosphere: if they weigh less than 50kg they are called "meteoroids", above that weight they are known as "asteroids."

THE ARBITRARY FOUNTAIN

Parco di Poggio Valicaia
6a,Via della Poggiona
50018 Scandicci (FI)
• http://www.comune.scandicci.fi.it/poggio_valicaia/index.htm
• Information: Ufficio parchi e qualità della vita urbana.
• Tel.: 055 75 91 247
• E-mail: parchieverde@comune.scandicci.fi.it
• Opening hours: from November to February, Saturday and Sunday 9.00-16.30; . March and October, Wednesday to Sunday 9.00-18.00; April, Wednesday to Sunday 9.00-20.00; May and September, Tuesday to Sunday 9.00-20.00; and June to August, Tuesday to Sunday 8.30-20.00.

A work of art with a will of its own...

About six metres high and made of iron and steel, the Arbitrary Fountain is the work of Gilberto Zorio (see below). At the top is a star-shaped container that collects rainwater and dew. When the liquid is at a certain level, the water is automatically ejected via a siphon. There is no telling when this might happen, so visitors can suddenly find themselves being doused with water. The creator's intention was to remind people that the laws of nature may be unpredictable and beyond human control.

The park itself is a haven of peace for the people of Florence, with various walks laid out to incorporate other works of art that are perfectly in keeping with the natural setting.

GILBERTO ZORIO

Gilberto Zorio est né en 1944 à Adorno Micca (Biella). Installé à Turin, il fut l'un des protagonistes du mouvement révolutionnaire des années 60 intitulé « Arte Povera » dont « l'attitude » consiste à défier l'industrie culturelle et la société de consommation selon une stratégie de guérilla. L'originalité de son œuvre est qu'elle est le plus souvent en action. L'une de ses œuvres les plus spectaculaires est appelée *Torcia* : des torches enflammées tombent sur l'œuvre pour la détruire.

Directions: At the exit from the Florence/Certosa motorway, turn left towards Florence. Go through Bottai and turn left at the traffic lights in the centre of Gallus. Take the next left onto the Volterrana, the road to Volterra (the P4). After just over 4 km, turn right onto the Romola road, immediately after the sign reading "*Chiesa Nova*." Follow this road for about 1km and then turn right onto the earthen track marked "Parco Poggio Valicaia." Another 1.5 km brings you to the car park. There, signposts indicate the various footpaths that lead to the fountain (a walk of about 20 minutes).

FORMER HOSPICE OF BIGALLO

14, Via Bigallo e Apparita. 50012 Bagno a Ripoli
- Visits by reservation at the Assessorato alla Cultura [Cultural Affairs Department] of Bagno a Ripoli
- Tel: 055 63 90 356
- Note that during the holiday season the first floor (used as hotel space) cannot be visited.
- Hotel Season: from 1 April to 30 September
- Hotel Reservations: Casella Postale 25. San Donato in Poggio. 50028 Tavarnelle val di Pesa
- Tel.: 340.41.23.101. E-Mail: info@bigallo.it. www.bigallo.it/bigost it.htm.
Manager: Franco Lodini: 335 39 30 50
- Rates (including breakfast): dormitory bed: 25 €; double room 39 € per person.
- Directions: By car, leave the Firenze Sud motorway and follow the signs to Bagno a Ripoli right to the sign indicating "Ospedale del Bigallo." By bus, take the no. 33 from the station of Santa Maria Novella and get off at the La Fonte stop. It is then a 15-minute walk.

A hotel in a former hospice

Located on the road to Arezzo and affording a remarkable panoramic view of Florence, the former Bigallo Hospice provided hospitality and assistance to pilgrimages on their way to Rome. Founded in the 13th century and modelled on a number of such hospices that were dotted around Europe, the Bigallo has now been carefully restored and can give you a real feel of what things must have been like eight centuries ago.

During the tourist season, visits are restricted to the ground floor because the first floor is actually still used to provide accommodation to guests. The first of the two dormitories is reminiscent of the sort of place one sees in films set in old-fashioned hospitals, with lines of beds separated from each other by a simple curtain. The other dormitory is a faithful reproduction of what the hospice was like at the time of the pilgrims; it is lined with a double podium on which mattresses are laid out

There are also five double rooms with en-suite bathrooms.

Still undergoing restoration, the ground floor has an attractive painted coffered ceiling. Halfway up the wall you can still see the rounded recess where a monk recited prayers during meals. The kitchen, which is open to visitors, is a spectacular sight with its fireplace, chimney canopy and stone sinks.

The rural charm of the site and the spectacular views it affords make this a wonderful place to stay.

THE FOUNTAIN OF FATA MORGANA

Corner of Via delle Fonti and Via di Fattucchia - 50012 Bagno a Ripoli
• Directions: By car, turn off the Firenze Sud motorway and follow the signs to
Greve in Chianti until you reach a place called Grassina. Follow Via delle Fonti, at
the beginning of which there is a signpost to the fountain, which stands at the far
end of the street.
• Visits by reservation only: Assessorato alla Cultura di Bagno a Ripoli (tel: 055 63
90 356) or Cooperativa per i Servizi Culturali Megaton (tel: 055 48 04 89)
• Admission: 2.60 €, reduced: 1.30 €
The building can be viewed from outside, but the interior and main fountain are
shut behind gates.

*A fountain
of eternal youth?*

The Fountain or Nymphaeum* of Fata Morgana (*Ninfeo della Fata Morgana*) is an astonishing building imbued with a dreamlike atmosphere of myth and, perhaps, magic. According to an inscription carved in stone**, the waters of this fountain are recognised as bestowing youth upon those who drink it. The unusual and mysterious look of the place has encouraged legends and stories: it is said that bacchanals were held here on summer nights, with beautiful young nymphs and fairies then disappearing just as suddenly as they had appeared. The whole structure was part of the gardens of the Villa Il Riposo which was built in the 15th century (it is also known as Villa Vecchietti, after the family who purchased the property in 1515). The grounds were not enclosed at the time as the fountain was originally intended for public use… in particular for the peasants working on the estate. Probably designed by Giambologna, the building is flanked by a tabernacle that dates from 1573-1574 and has two drinking-fountains and a water-trough for animals. The central fountain is known as *Il Fonte del Viandante* [Fountain of the Traveller] because it was available to any passers-by. The basin is surmounted by a strange sculpture of a gorgon, which is said to depict Fata Morgana. The body of the building gives access to the main fountain. This has a shell-shaped basin supported by two mermaids. The niche above it is rather bare as another statue of Fata Morgana – also the work of Giambologna – has now disappeared.

FATA MORGANA

According to legend, Fata Morgana was King Arthur's sister (or half-sister), also known as Morgan le Fay. She tried to resist the growing power of Christianity within Brittany, which was largely due to the influence of the very pious Queen Gweniver. Ancient beliefs were the basis of her own magical powers, as they were at the basis of the powers wielded by Merlin. It was Morgana who is said to have embroidered the magical scabbard for Excalibur, which protected Arthur from any fatal wound in combat.

---

* In Roman times a nymphaeum was a monumental public fountain adorned with sculpture
and jets of waters. It was made up of one or more basins backed by a multi-level ornamental
façade. There were also private nymphaea, for example in Pompeii. Originally, the term came
from Greek and referred to a sanctuary dedicated to the nymphs.

** "I am, o reader, the youthful Fata Morgana, who here gives youth to others…."

STATUE OF FIDO

②③

Piazza Dante
50032 Borgo San Lorenzo

> **After the death of his owner, Fido waited at the same spot for 14 years...**

Curiously, the main square in Borgo San Lorenzo features the statue of a dog, which bears the inscription "To Fido, an example of fidelity." The story began when Carlo Soriano found a wounded and abandoned dog that he gave the typical name of "Fido." Unfortunately, their time together was cut short when Carlo was killed during a bombing raid on 30 December 1943. From that day onwards, Fido would for fourteen years (that is, more than 5,000 days) continue to go to the bus stop of Luco del Mugello to await his owner's return from work at the factory.

A campaign started by a journalist would ultimately lead to the town's mayor presenting Fido with a Gold Medal in a ceremony held on 9 November 1957 in the presence of Carlo Soriano's widow. Fido died on 9 June 1958 and was buried alongside his master.

SIGHTS NEARBY:

CRUCIFIX IN THE ORATORY OF THE SANCTISSIMO CROCIFISSO DI MIRACOLI **②④**

Piazza G. Pecori Giraldi
50032 Borgo San Lorenzo (FI)
The Crucifix is displayed on every Friday in Lent, on Easter Sunday and the first Sunday of each month.
For further information, phone 055 84 59 088

Undoubtedly the work of the 14th century sculptor Giovanni Pisano, this painted wood crucifix is, as the name of the oratory suggests, miraculous. Located in a niche above the main altar it is usually hidden by a painting by the 19th century artist Giuseppe Bezzuoli and is only rarely put on display (see dates above), with the painting being raised by a special mechanism. In the 15th century a group of German pilgrims who had bought the wooden crucifix to take to Rome were caught up in an outbreak of the plague and had to leave it behind in Borgo San Lorenzo. This Cross was then acquired by a confraternity of flagellants and soon became renowned for its miraculous powers. Initially housed at the premises of the confraternity, it was later moved to this oratory, which was built over the period 1714-1743. Amongst other things, the crucifix is credited with having put an end to an outbreak of the plague in the fifteenth century, with the fact that the village suffered only slight damage during the earth tremors of 1542 (however, after the 1919 earthquake, the oratory did have to be entirely rebuilt) and, finally, with the end of the French occupation in 1799.

SIENA

STRANGE "LAMPPOST" IN VIA DEL REFE NERO ❶

21, Via del Refe Nero

A head on a spike in a cage

At no. 21 Via del Refe Nero there is a very mysterious sight: a severed head fixed on a spike and enclosed within a cage of wrought iron. This macabre decoration was set up by the previous owner, the Sienese antiquarian Giuseppe Mazzoni. In effect, he restructured this entire Palazzo del Diavolo Rosso [Palace of the Red Devil] in the 1930s, giving it a rather fanciful neo-medieval appearance.

Mazzoni was an eccentric character who inherited from his father, another passionate collector, the family business of Casa d'Arte Antica Senese, which had been founded in 1880. After his retirement, Giuseppe Mazzoni would acquire a certain notoriety in the 1950s when, in *Il Giornale dell'Antiquario* [The Antique Dealer's Journal], he published an account of the role he had played in selling the "works" of the gifted forger Icilio Federico Joni (1866-1946).

A FORGER OF GENIUS

Between 1890 and 1918, Icilio Federico Joni would manage to pass off a number of his own creations as the works of such 14th and 15th century Sienese masters as Duccio, Lorenzetti and Martini. Even experts of the calibre of Bernard Berenson were taken in by his almost perfect copies.

A foundling, Joni had been raised at the Santa Maria della Scala orphanage. His autobiography *Le Memorie di un pittore di quadri antichi* [Memoirs of a Painter of Old Masters] was published in 1932. Even though it disguised the names of the dealers who had sold his paintings, it had an enormous impact, creating uncertainty for all the private individuals and public institutions that had purchased a work by the Siena Primitives during the period when Icilio Federico Joni was active as a forger.

SIGHTS NEARBY:

A PLAQUE COMMEMORATING THE REFORM OF THE CALENDAR ❷

Façade of the Palazzo Pubblico - Piazza del Campo

On 20 November 1749, the Grand Duke of Tuscany decreed that, from 1 January the following year, there was to be one uniform calendar used within his duchy. Known as the "modern style" [stile *moderno*] calendar, it replaced the "incarnation calendars" that had previously been used in Pisa and Florence. These latter not only celebrated the New Year on 23 March (the Feast of the Annunciation; hence the reference to "incarnation"), but also were also at variance with one another: the Pisan calendar was 9 months and 7 days ahead of the "modern" version, while the Florentine calendar lagged 2 months and 24 days behind. At the time of the reform, Siena was using the Florentine calendar.

A CHRIST WITH MOVEABLE ARMS

Basilica of San Francesco
Piazza San Francesco
53100 Siena (SI)
• Opening hours: 7.30-12.00 and 15.30-19.00.
In winter, closed from "around" 19.00.
• Free admission.

> *A Christ with moving limbs*

There are not many existing statues of Christ with moving arms and limbs; most of them were suppressed by the ecclesiastical authorities during the period of the Reformation and, particularly, the Counter-Reformation. The majority of such statues were medieval in origin and had been used primarily during Holy Week, when they figured in realistic enactments of the Deposition from the Cross (a episode of Christ's Passion that was known in Italy as Il Mortorio). Such enactments were even more popular in Spain and can still be seen today in some countries of South America: at San Andres Sajeabaja in Guatemala, for example, a Christ with moveable limbs is removed from the Cross each Good Friday and laid out in a glass coffin. The main feature of these figures is an articulated shoulder joint. This means the arms can be raised when fixing Christ to the Cross, and then hang limp after the nails are removed. A further advantage was that the arms could be raised to any angle, so that the body could be adapted to any type of cross.

There is no precise information as to the origin or date of this particular example of a Christ with moveable arms. Possibly it is contemporary with that in the church of San Pietro de Pieve in Presciano (Valdarno), which has been dated from the 15th century. Note that the figure of Christ in Presciano may be difficult to see, as the church there is only open for mass and other religious services.

SIGHTS NEARBY:

THE HERALDIC ARMS OF THE TOLOMEI FAMILY

Entering the cloister to the right of the basilica, if you turn left and walk to the far end you come to a staircase whose steps are adorned with a number of little coats-of-arms: however, you need good eyesight to make them out. Tradition has

it that these eighteen identical crests of the Tolomei commemorate the eighteen members of that family who were murdered in the 14th century during the course of a meal held at a vlla in Via Cassia; the event was supposed to ark their reconciliation with the Salimbeni family. This tragic episode would lead to the entire area becoming known as Malamerenda from the Italian words for evil/bad [male] and meal/refreshment [merenda].

❺

SIGHTS NEARBY:

SAINT CATHERINE'S TEETH

The steps linking Piazza San Giovanni and Piazza Jacopo della Quercia
53100 Siena (SI)

Legend has it that the small holes in the steps behind the Baptistery leading up to the cathedral esplanade and the Ospedale di Santa Maria della Scala are actually the toothmarks of St. Catherine of Siena herself. While running one day to the hospital where she cared for the sick, the saint was tripped up by the Devil and is said to have lost all her teeth…making these marks in the marble when she fell. However, historical dates ruthlessly put paid to this charming little anecdote: the steps were, in fact, built by Giovanni Sabatelli in 1451, some 70 years after the death of St. Catherine. When she was alive, the steps here were simply beaten earth.

SAINT CATHERINE

Born in Siena on 25 March 1347, Catherine Benincasa, who could not write and did not know any Latin, would paradoxically leave a substantial body of work treasured by the Church. Having taken a vow of chastity, she fasted to a point that was regarded as excessive even in medieval times; her acts of extreme penitence included the wearing of a hair shirt and of a belt lined with iron tacks that cut into her flesh. In 1367 Jesus, in the company of his holy mother and saints, is said to have appeared to her to ask for her hand in marriage. Then, in 1368, after Christ placed a ruby ring on the woman's finger to mark this mystical union, Catherine would experience a succession of raptures that continued uninterruptedly for a whole week. Though that ring was visible only to the saint herself, it is often part of her iconography – together with the lilies that symbolise her chastity. Tradition has it that Catherine then received the marks of the stigmata on 1 April 1375 whilst she was praying in the church of St. Christine of Pisa; however, no one ever saw those marks upon her body. In 1377 she convinced Pope Gregory XI to leave Avignon for Italy. She died in Rome some three years later, at the age of 33 (29 April 1380).

St. Catherine is the patron saint of Italy, of journalists, and of the media (including the Internet). She is also one of the patron saints of Europe (see below).

THE MIRACULOUS RETURN OF SAINT CATHERINE'S HEAD

When St. Catherine died in Rome, the people of Siena were anxious to have her earthly remains returned to her home city. The Romans had other ideas, and so a delegation was sent from Siena in 1384. As it proved impossible to persuade the Romans, or to seize the saint's body in its entirety, these emissaries cut off her head and put it in a sack. When the guards on duty stopped them and asked them to open the bag, hundreds of rose petals flew out… But once the delegation got back to Siena, the saint's head materialised once again. It is now housed in a chapel in the basilica of San Domenico. This charming story does not however explain how St. Catherine's right thumb comes to be in Siena … or how her foot got to Venice (where it is today housed in the Basilica of San Giovanni e Paolo).

MAGIC SQUARE IN THE CATHEDRAL ❻

Siena Cathedral
Piazza del Duomo
53100 Siena (SI)
• www.operaduomo.siena.it/
• Opening hours: 1 March to 31 May, weekdays 10.30-19.30, Sundays and holidays 13.30-17.30; 1 June to 31 August, weekdays, Sundays, and holidays 13.30-18.00; 1 September to 1 November, weekdays, Sundays, and holidays 13.30-17.30; 2 November to 28 February, weekdays, Sundays, and holidays 13.30-17.30.
• Admission: 3 €.

Secret identity codes for the first Christians

O On the left side of the cathedral, on practically the last part of the wall that is visible, there is a strange square formed of five Latin words carved into a slab of white marble. Arranged one word per line, these form a palindrome which reads:

SATOR   AREPO   TENET   OPERA   ROTAS

Read left to right, right to left, upwards or downwards, this arrangement of letters always forms the same sentence: Sator arepo tenet opera rotas. There are some doubts about the meaning of arepo, but the two translations for the entire phrase most widely accepted are: "The Sower takes care of his plough and his work" or "The Labourer guiding the plough works by turning around." All sorts of esoteric, religious, alchemical, numerological and cabbalistic interpretations of these sentences have been put forward; however, the hypothesis that the stone is somehow linked with the Templars became untenable when, in 1936, a similar stone palindrome was found on a column in the amphitheatre of Pompeii, the Roman city buried by an eruption of Vesuvius in 79 AD.

Nevertheless, a Christian explanation of its origin still seems to be the most plausible one, with this square of words being used by the early Christians as a code whereby they could recognise each other. Note, for example, that the square contains a central cross made up of the word TENET, flanked at top and bottom by the letters A and O, Alpha and Omega. What is more, one can form a cross with the 25 letters and form the words Pater noster twice, without using the A and the O twice... It could be that these palindromes or "magic squares" or "holy squares" were intended to drive the forces of evil away from the cathedral (a function similar to that of the labyrinth at the cathedral of Lucca, see page 177).

Such magic squares are to be found in about a dozen places in Italy, most notably at Campiglia Marittima outside Livorno (see page 245), at the Palazzo Benciolini in Verona and in Urbino.

SHAFTS FROM THE MONTAPERTI "VICTORY CHARIOT"

Cathedral of Santa Maria Assunta
Piazza del Duomo
53100 Siena (SI)

Two unusual reminders of the battle of Montaperti inside the Cathedral

Placed vertically behind the fifth columns in the nave of the cathedral are two reminders of the famous victory of Montaperti (see below). They look just like two poles of wood, but they are in fact the shafts from the Victory Chariot (*carroccio*) and were placed here as an offering of thanks to the Madonna degli Occhi Grossi [Madonna of the Large Eyes] that then stood on the high altar of the cathedral. (It is now to be seen in the Museo dell'Opera Metropolitana, a short distance away).

On the eve of the battle, the entire city went in solemn procession with this *carroccio* to invoke the protection of the Madonna. Indeed, the very survival of the vehicle after the battle was itself a sort of miracle. It had been entrusted to the Luccan troops led by Niccolò da Bigozzi, who were thrown into disarray when their captain was impaled by the German knight Gualtieri d'Astimbergh. In the ensuing confusion, Bigozzi's troops became involved in the battle itself and forgot their orders to protect the venerated *carroccio*.

THE BATTLE OF MONTAPERTI

The battle of Montaperti was the culmination of the war between Siena and Florence in the 13th century, when economic and political rivalry made a clash between the two cities inevitable. Furthermore, Florence was a Guelph city supporting the Papacy, whilst Siena was Ghibelline and supported the Holy Roman Emperor.

The casus belli exploited by the Florentines on this occasion was the fact that Siena had given refuge to the Ghibellines who had just been driven out of Florence. The battle took place on 4 September 1260. Over the years, accounts of the battle became more legendary than factual, attributing the Sienese victory to feats of arms that are still the subject of discussion and debate.

The term "Guelph" comes from the name of the German dynasty of the Welfs. It refers to the faction who supported the pope in opposition to the Holy Roman Emperor. The term "Ghibelline" comes from the name of the castle of Waiblingen in Germany, the seat of the Hohenstaufen dynasty, who struggled to establish themselves on the throne of the Holy Roman Empire.

MARKS OF GUNFIRE ON THE NEW CATHEDRAL ❽

Facciatone
Piazza Jacopo della Quercia

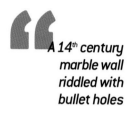

A 14th century marble wall riddled with bullet holes

On the imposing facade of the (unfinished) new cathedral, there are dozens of bullet holes in the marble. Siena was liberated on 3 July 1944, but in the last days of June a plane (no one knew if it was American or German) made several low passes here, strafing the area around the cathedral. Many of the bullets then ricocheted off the ground and hit the façade of the church. It was later discovered that the pilot was actually from Siena (he lived in Via di Rossi) and had wanted to demonstrate that the Fascist army still had the power to strike back.

A WELCOME LESS WARM THAN IT SEEMS...

The arch over the Camolia gateway bears the welcoming inscription *Cor magis tibi Sena pandit* [Siena opens its heart to you even wider than its gates], which was carved there in honour of Ferdinando I de Medici when he visited the city. The phrase figures in all the tourist books, but most of the local people know that it was far from being a spontaneous expression of welcome... Cosimo I, known in Siena as the "Medicean thief," had just robbed the city of its liberty...

THE CONTRADA MUSEUMS

The city's various *contrada* [districts], which compete against one another every year in the famous Palio, each have their own church and museum. Some of the museums are less interesting than others (primarily because of the dull modern buildings which house them), but some are as beautiful as the local church. However, outside the period of the Palio, it is difficult to gain access to any of them, with phone calls getting switched to fax machines and e-mails simply going unanswered.

For those who do manage to visit them, the museums of the La Selva, La Girafe and La Licorne *contrade* are fascinating; each of these districts also has a beautiful church. In the La Girafe museum (18, Via delle Vergini. Tel: 0577 28 70 91) there is the victory banner from the 1967 Palio, which was stolen by some pranksters from Bologna. The whole incident caused an uproar. Even when the culprits returned the banner, they were warned not to hang around; the people of Siena took a very poor view of such "jokes." The museum of the *Contrada della Licorna* (church of San Giorgio, 15 Via di Follonica. Tel: 0577-288549 and 0577 49298) contains "La Martinella," the bell seized from the Florentine victory chariot (*carroccio*) at the battle of Montaperti in 1260 (see previous two pages).

THE WINDOWS IN PIAZZA DI POSTIERLA ❾

Piazza di Postierla
Quattro Cantoni

The smallest window in the world?

Placed beneath normal windows, these tiny finestrelle were intended to allow children to watch what was happening the street below without any danger of falling out (see the finestrelle in Volterra, page 129 and Lucca, page 189). The finestrella in Piazza di Postierla even has its own charming little shutters. The Siena city council even claims that this is "the smallest window in the world."

SIGHTS NEARBY:

A PLAQUE WARNING OFF PROSTITUTES ❿

Corner of Via del Castelvecchio and Via San Pietro

The house on this street corner has a curious plaque dating from 1704. It warns that prostitutes, even if they are married, cannot take up residence in Via Castelvecchio, on pain of a fine of 10 scudi for any infringement.

The street's name is a reference to the old castle that was the medieval core around which the city grew. Some remains of the old ramparts can be seen in the first house on the right.

THE MADONNA OF THE CROW ⓫

2, Via del Castelvecchio

At the corner of Via Stalloreggi and Via del Castelvecchio is a tabernacle with frescoes by Giovanni Antonio Bazzi , known as Il Sodoma*. A pietà, with the Virgin holding the dead Christ in her arms, the fresco is known in Siena as The Madonna of the Crow. The name itself dates from 1348, when a crow that fell dead in front of the tabernacle was taken as a presage of the arrival in Siena of the plague that had been raging in Europe for almost a year.

The Black Death would in fact soon arrive from Pisa, being particularly virulent in the months from April to October 1348. The Sienese chronicler Agnolo di Tura described it as "the worst, the grimmest and most horrible that the city has known. Everyone expected to die. The church bells no longer rang. It was the end of the world..." He himself lost his five children during the outbreak.

It was ultimately impossible to count the number of victims; but it is estimated that two-thirds of a population of 100,000 were affected.

---

* Sodoma's nickname was a mocking reference to his taste for youths...

◀ **SIGHTS NEARBY:**

THE GHOST IN THE BOTANICAL GARDEN: ⓬

The marble bust of the painter Giacomo del Sodoma

50, Via della Cerchia

The curious marble head embedded in the wall of the house at 50, Via della Cerchia is said to be a portrait bust of the painter Giacomo del Sodoma , known as Giomo (1507-1562), who is not to be confused with Giovanni Antonio Bazzi, known as Il Sodoma (1477-1549). Popular tradition links this bust with the ghost which made nocturnal appearances in the Botanical Gardens at the beginning of the 20th century.

In his Toscanissima (Edizioni Bonecchi), Giorgio Batini claims, however, that the head is that of "the hermit of Porta dell'Arco," a young nobleman who fought against the Florentines at the battle of Montalcino in 1176. Seriously wounded during that defeat, he is said to have recovered after a long convalescence, at the end of which he decided to abandon military glory for life as a hermit at the city gateway of Porta all'Arco. However, when the Sienese marched out to fight again in 1207, he joined them, only to be killed during the first skirmishes with the Florentines.

On 9 November 1952, this ghostly visage would once more be the subject of talk — when the bust in Via della Cerchia disappeared. One evening, perhaps after a drink too many over dinner, the members of the Contrada de la Tartuca [tortoise] had decided they wanted to take a closer look at this symbolic head. The street being badly lit, they took it home with them so as to be able to see it properly. Then they forgot to put it back, and the press got hold of the story. However, the "Hermit of Porta dell'Arco" was then discreetly returned to its niche — and the furore soon subsided.

16 JUNE 1794: A HAIL OF METEORITES ON SIENA

At 7pm on 16 June 1794 meteorites rained down on the south-eastern part of the city of Siena. It was the first time in recorded history that such a shower had fallen within an urban area, making it possible for the phenomenon to be studied. The meteorites were preceded by a dense cloud issuing plumes of smoke and slow gleams of red lightning. Those which struck the ground varied in weight from a few hundred milligrams to three kilos. There were numerous eyewitnesses, including a number of English tourists (already!). The event then attracted sightseers as well as scientists from all over Italy, who wanted to collect testimonies before putting forward any explanations. Just 18 hours after this meteorite shower, the volcano Vesuvius erupted. The scientific community was divided into two camps, between those who thought the two events were connected and those who did not; the volcano is, after all, 450 kilometres from Siena. By an incredible coincidence, just two months before the meteorites fell, the German physicist Ernst Chaladni had published his The Origin of Ferrous Rocks, in which he argued that they could have fallen out of the sky. The publication of this work in Great Britain — together with the fall of a rock weighing 30 kg in Yorkshire and eyewitness accounts from those who might earlier have kept quiet for fear of being ridiculed — helped to advance serious scientific study of meteorites.

THE NATURAL HISTORY MUSEUM OF THE ACCADEMIA DEGLI FISIOCRITICI*

❶❸

2, Piazzetta Silvio Gigli - 53100 Siena (SI)
• Tel/Fax. : 0577 47 002 • E-mail : fisiocritici@unisi.it
• www.accademiafisiocritici.it
The internet site offers a very detailed "virtual tour" comprising a remarkable number of videos and abundant PDF files.
• Opening hours: 9.00-13.00 and 15.00-18.00. Closed Thursday afternoon, Saturday, Sunday and holidays.
• Free admission.

Founded more than 300 years ago, the Academy of the Physiocritics has various collections which form a museum with a distinct 19th century charm. Since 1816 this has been housed in a

> **The atmosphere of a wunderkammer**

12th century monastery, with its numerous remarkable exhibits divided between three main sections: geological, zoological and anatomical. At the centre of the cloister, for example, is the skeleton of a 15-metre whale which became beached near Piombino in 1974.

In the geological section, be sure not to miss the collection of ancient marbles. The 230 samples come from buildings not only in Rome and the surrounding area but from all the various regions of the Roman Empire. The section also includes one of the world's most famous meteorites, known as the "Siena Meteorite:" this chondrite (the name indicates a meteorite of which at least 35% is made up of metals) was one of those which fell on the city in the famous meteorite storm of 16 June 1794 (see previous double page).

Among the other curiosities of this fascinating museum are the display cases of monsters, including two-headed lambs and sheep. Under a black cloth cover there is even part of the coat of a mammoth found frozen in Siberia. Moving into the screening room, one also finds a magnificent meridian now laid out under the spectators' seats. The work of Giuseppe Pianigiani, this is a detailed reconstruction of the original designed and created in 1703 by the founder of the Academy, Pirro Maria Gabrielli. At the time, this meant that Siena was one of only four cities with such an instrument (the others being Paris, Rome and Bologna). The instrument worked in this way: a guardian used to watch for the exact passage of a ray of sunlight along the axis of the meridian and then immediately have the bell (in the Torre della Mangia) rung to announce noon. The sundial was even used to correct mechanical clocks. Known as the "Physiocritic Heliometre," it was unfortunately destroyed during an earthquake in 1798.

* The word "physiocritic" comes from the Greek words physis (Nature) and kritikos (he who studies).

PALAZZO GALGANO

47, Via Roma

> A metal ring that recalls something

With reference to the Abbey of Galgano and the sword in the stone (see page 127), the rings at Palazzo Galgano to which riders used to tie their horses are modelled on that famous sword; they, too, appear to be sunk into the stone. In fact, the palazzo was built for the monks from that abbey in 1474, when what is now Via Roma was called Via Maddalena.

SIGHTS NEARBY:

THE RUSTY PLAQUES OF THE OLD PSYCHIATRIC HOSPITAL

56, Via Roma
53100 Siena (SI)

Easy to make out thanks to the monumental portal that stands at the beginning of Via Roma, the old psychiatric hospital now houses part of the university. However, there are some extant traces of the *città della follia* [city of madness] that was once located here. Founded at the end of the 19th century, the hospital applied the theories of its day, which saw work as the essential basis for the treatment of mentally ill patients. It was laid out as a small town, with streets, workshops and shops – a "protected space" within which the inmates were allowed to move freely. Today, one still finds here and there a rusty plaque indicating the name of street or the presence of a tobacconist's.

A PAINTING IN EXCHANGE FOR FREEDOM

MARCOVALDO'S *VIRGIN AND CHILD*

Basilica di Santa Maria dei Servi

Piazza Alessandro Manzoni

The altarpiece in the second chapel along the south wall of the basilica was painted in 1261 by Coppo di Marcovaldo (1225-1265) and depicts The Virgin and Child with Two Angels. The circumstances in which this was created are worth mentioning. Fighting on the Florentine side in the battle of Montaperti in 1260 (see page 111), Coppo di Marcovaldo was taken prisoner by the Sienese. As he had no money to ransom himself, he was offered a deal which, tradition has it, was proposed in this terse exchange:

"What can you do?... Paint?... So paint!"

And this was how Coppo di Marcovaldo's only signed work comes to be found in the Basilica dei Servi.

MUSEUM OF THE CONFRATERNITÀ DI SANTA MARIA IN PORTICO

Via Fontegiusta
53100 Siena (SI)
• Visits by appointment only: phone Silvano Carletti at 347 181 31 14.
• Admission is free, but a contribution to the costs of maintaining and restoring the church is appreciated.

Church of Santa Maria in Portico
• Mass each weekday at 8.00, open until noon; Saturday open at 17.00 with mass at 18.30; Sunday mass at 10.30.

> *The trophies of Christopher Columbus*

A discreet little place with no public signs to announce its presence, the museum of the Confraternità di Santa Maria in Portico is one of the gems of Siena. It can be visited only by appointment, when you enjoy an informed guided tour in the company of Silvano Carletti, a passionate student of his city's art and history. Along with priestly robes, ancient church furnishings, and other precious objects that are here protected against theft, one will also find four mementoes which, tradition has it, were offered by Christopher Columbus himself while still a student at Siena University. Said to have fallen in love with a young woman who was a parishioner of Fontegiusta, the young man presented the church with a painted wooden shield, an arquebus butt, a helmet, and sword – all of them supposed to be trophies from the battle of Poggio Imperiale fought against the Florentines in 1479.

The museum also has other curiosities relating to the life of the confraternity. These include some black and white beans which are over 200 years old and were found recently in an old coffer. The beans were not to be eaten but served as markers when the confraternity Council voted: a white bean meant "yes," a black one "no."

> The museum and the church after which it is named are often referred to by the name of the district, Fontegiusta, which itself is named after a drinking fountain. The objects described above once hung in the church itself, just below the oculus of the façade. All that remains there now is the spectacular whale bone, which was also donated by Christopher Columbus

SIGHTS NEARBY:

COLUMN COMMEMORATING THE MEETING OF FREDERICK III AND ELEANOR OF PORTUGAL

The curious column in Piazza Amedola commemorates the remarkable episode of the first meeting between Frederick III, Holy Roman Emperor, and his betrothed, Eleanor, Infanta of Portugal. The two had never seen each other before, and this meeting was organised by the then bishop of Siena, Enea Silvio Piccolomini, later Pope Pius II (see Pienza page 145). Remarkably, Pinturrichio's fresco of the event in the Piccolomini Library within the cathedral already shows the presence of a commemorative column, although the encounter had only taken place a few years before...

OUTSIDE SIENA

MUMMIFIED HANDS OF A THIEF

Abbey of San Galgano and the Montesiepi Chapel
53012 Chiusdino (SI)
• Free access to the abbey
• The chapel is open from 9.30 to dusk. No charge for admission
• Tel: 0577 75 67 38

*An unidentified
mummy
and a famous
sword*

One of the sights that no visitor to Tuscany should miss, the Abbey of San Galgano is famous the world over: the esoteric symbolism of the sword in the stone, the serene beauty of an abbey which now stands open to the sky, and the powerful legends associated with the place – all make this a "must" for lovers of the curious and the usual. The hermitage (eremo in Italian) where the body of St. Galgano lies is on the top of the small hill, while the most spectacular feature of the abbey – the sword in the stone – is now protected by a dome of plexiglas.

However, the most curious feature of the entire place is to be found in the chapel alongside this sword: a coffer of wrought iron whose contents are hidden from the eyes of the young and the sensitive by a deep red cloth. When you lift the covering, beneath it you'll see two mummified forearms, the hands twisted in pain. A panel under the coffer explains that these belonged to one of the three men who, in 1181, tried to steal San Galgano's sword. Not only did they fail to get the sword, but they fell victim to wolves who protected the saint's hermitage. Though the story strikes one as mythical, recent carbon-dating has shown that the limbs do in fact date from the 12th century, the era in which the saint lived.

THE SWORD IN THE STONE The legend of saint Galgano

Galgano Guidotti (1148 – 1181) was born into a noble family in Chiusdino, the village which stands alongside the abbey. Initially he led a carefree and dissolute life, which was brought to an end when the angel Gabriel appeared to him, exhorting him to mend his ways. In 1180 Galgano became a Cistercian monk, and marked the rejection of his former life by breaking his sword against a rock. However, instead of shattering, the sword sank into the stone, becoming more like a cross than a weapon – a "transformation" which Galgano interpreted as a sign from God. He would then live the rest of his days as a hermit. There are those who doubt the authenticity of the sword now on display. But it might be best to keep such doubts from children...

GRAFFITI IN THE FORMER PSYCHIATRIC BUILDING OF SAN GIROLAMO

❷

Ferri Building - Borgata San Lazzaro
56048 Volterra (PI)

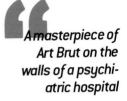

A masterpiece of Art Brut on the walls of a psychiatric hospital

In the 1960s, Oreste Fernando Nannetti – who renamed himself "N.O.F.4" – created one of the world's masterpieces of Art Brut on the walls of the Ferri building in the old psychiatric hospital. Over a stretch of wall measuring 180x2m, Nannetti used the buckle of the belt from his patient's uniform to write – or, rather, draw – his "Book of Life." Whilst certain lines of the script are now indecipherable, most can be made out – even if they are as hermetic as the Etruscan script they so strangely resemble.

Born in Rome in 1927, Nannetti would die in 1994. A withdrawn and taciturn person, he spoke to no one apart from a psychiatric nurse (Aldo Trafeli), who understood that Nannetti was not simply mad but rather devoting himself to an artistic project that lay well outside the usual realms of sanity. Nannetti worked so furiously on his scratchings that the dust from the stone caused serious damage to his eyes. Nowadays, his work is gradually disappearing and the old hospital buildings are threatened with redevelopment.

The treatment of mental patients and the work of NOF4' inspired the singer-songwriter Simone Cristicchi to write *Ti regalerò una rosa* [I will give you a rose], which won first prize at the 2007 San Remo Song Festival.

> For visits, apply to the management of the new hospital:
> U.O. Direzione amministrativa AVC. Dotoressa Sabina Ghilli. 5, Borgata San Lazzaro.
> 56048 Volterra - E-mail: s.ghilli@usl5.toscana.it

SIGHTS NEARBY:

CHILDREN'S WINDOWS AT 36 VIA RICCIARELLI

❸

These small *finestrelle* were designed to allow young children to satisfy their legitimate curiosity about the outside world without any risk of falling to the ground below. The palazzo that runs from 34 to 38 Via Ricciarelli is particularly noteworthy because every single normal window is accompanied by its *finestrella*. At no. 6 Via Buonparenti there is also an old *buchetta*.

MEDIEVAL STANDARD MEASURES

❹

Palazzo dei Priori, Piazza dei Priori. Porta San Francesco, Via S. Lino

In Volterra one can still see two traces of the systems of measurement used in medieval times. Incised horizontally upon the stone facade of Palazzo dei Priori is a standard measure of the *canna volterrana* (2.362 metres), a unit of measurement in use in the 13th century. On the inner wall to the right of the San Francesco gate – also known as the San Stefano or Pisan gate – is a standard *canna pisana*. Slightly longer than the *canna volterrana*, this is carved into the stone vertically here. These standard measures were used when there was any dispute between merchants and their customers.

SIGHTS NEARBY:

A CANNONBALL EMBEDDED IN A FAÇADE

12, Via Franceschini.

Volterra

At no. 12 Via Franceschini (formerly Via del Campanile) there is a cannonball embedded in the façade of a building. If asked, the locals say either that they know nothing about it or else describe it as "yet another Florentine cannonball."

TUSCANY: THE FIRST STATE IN THE WORLD TO ABOLISH THE DEATH PENALTY

Town Hall. 18, Via Campana. 53034 Colle di Val d'Elsa (Siena).

The plaque is on the right in the corridor leading from the entrance to the ground-floor hall. It was unveiled on 30 November 2000, the 214th anniversary of the abolition.

Acting upon the advice of the criminologist Cesare Beccaria, Pietro Leopoldo I of Tuscany signed a decree abolishing the death penalty and torture on 30 November 1786, making Tuscany the first country to do so. Reintroduced in 1790 for the crime of insurrection against the state, the penalty would later (29 August 1817) be further extended by Grand Duke Ferdinand III to cover crimes against common law (see Montepescali, page 282). However, that decision was made during the period of reactionary restoration that followed the fall of Napoleon and the Congress of Vienna. In 1859 the provisional government of Tuscany would abolish the death penalty for good. The kingdom of Italy later adopted the abolition in 1889, with a nearly unanimous vote by the two elected chambers of parliament, but in fact the penalty had not been used since the general amnesty decreed by Umberto I of Savoia on 18 January 1878. Executions, however, were still permitted under the military penal code and the death penalty continued to be applied in the Italian colonies. In 1926 the Fascist government reintroduced the death penalty for attempts on the life of members of the royal family or the head of state, as well as for crimes against national security. The Constitution of the Italian Republic voted on 27 December 1947 would then finally abolish the death penalty... in peace time. It remained part of the military penal code until 1994.

SAN GIMIGNANO: TORTURE CAPITAL OF THE WORLD...

Three museums dedicated to torture, execution and suffering! The inhabitants of this town of fine medieval towers seem quite happy with the image this gives of the place.

A visit to all three museums is not something for the faint-hearted... or for those on a tight family budget (for some reason, children seem to love these sorts of places). The first museum, in Piazza della Cisterna, is the oldest. It was founded in 1983 and has the most "intimate" atmosphere. The exhibits range from a guillotine to the "Iron Maiden" (a metal figure with a female head, this is lined with hard iron spikes). There are also various refinements upon the theme of impaling. Something for all the family! The second museum, in Via San Giovanni, seems to be run by same group that operates the Interactive Museum of Medieval Florence. Its waxwork figures are terrifyingly realistic.

As for the Museum of Executions, it is rather ironic that this is located within the territory of the state which, in 1786, would become the first in the world to abolish the death penalty (see above).

Museum of Torture – 1/3, Via del Castello
Museum of Torture – 15, Via San Giovanni
Museum of Executions – 123, Via San Giovanni

ANTHROPOMORPHIC EX-VOTOS
AT THE SANCTUARY OF ROMITUZZO

17, Via P. Burresi
53036 Poggibonsi (Siena)
• Tel: 0577 93 80 71

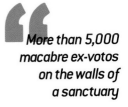

More than 5,000 macabre ex-votos on the walls of a sanctuary

This amazing place takes its name from the female hermits that used to pray here in the 14th century (romituzzo means "little hermitage"). Initially a small tabernacle with an image of the Madonna stood on this spot, the chapel then being built in 1460.

From the 16th century onwards an increasing number of miracles were attributed to the Madonna of Romituzzo, leading to the custom of placing anthropomorphic ex-votos here in thanks for grace received. Made of papier-mâché by the craftsmen of the Colle di Val d'Elsa, they depicted the part of the body which had been saved or cured thanks to the intercession of the Virgin.

Many of these ex-votos were destroyed during a fire in 1631; however, 5,125 still remain. Lining the walls of the chapel, they give the place a rather surrealistic air. The body parts include: 1,400 heads, 1,171 legs, 559 feet, 550 hands, 425 arms, 278 torsos and 192 faces. There are also 351 profiles and 182 babies.

MAXIMILIAN'S VOLTERRA CANDELABRAS ARE YET TO BE PAID FOR

A private home, Palazzo Viti can however be visited, sometimes with amusing information and facts being supplied by Giovanna Viti, who still lives here. One should note that the family crest does not include the royal crown: Vittorio-Emanuele II was received here, but as the unifier of Italy rather than as a reigning sovereign. The Viti are staunchly republican aristocrats.

In the first main room, known as the ballroom, there are two surprisingly large and magnificent alabaster candelabras. They were original made for the ill-fated Maximilian of Habsburg, who would – briefly – reign as Maximilian I, Emperor of Mexico. When he was executed in 1867, the candelabras had still not been paid for, causing substantial losses to a number of alabaster craftsmen in Volterra; Giuseppe Viti himself would be forced into bankruptcy partly because of this unpaid debt.

There are also two display cases with a unique collection of the broth cups used by women who had just given birth; the broth in question was supposed to stimulate their milk for breast-feeding. Quite apart from these curiosities, Palazzo Viti is in itself a fascinating place – above all for those who have seen Luchino Visconti's Sandra, starring Claudia Cardinale and Jean Sorel.

Palazzo Viti. 41, Via dei Sarti. Volterra. Tel: 0588 84 047. Opening hours: from 10.00-13.00 and 14.30-18.30 during the high season. Out of season, by appointment: call Consorzio Turistico Volterra (0588 86 099) or the palazzo itself (see number above). Admission: 4 €.

THE FROG FOUNTAIN IN GAIOLE IN CHIANTI ❻

Via Padre Cristoforo Chiantini
San Sano
53013 Gaiole in Chianti (SI)

> *A wine-drinking frog...*

This fountain has a very unusual statue of a frog gulping down wine. Even more curiously, the statue owes its existence to a television programme.

In the 1967 programme *Tappabuchi* , a word that might be translated as "stopgap," the presenter Corrado offered prizes for contestants who could dance, sing, recite poems or even imitate animals. One contestant from San Sano, Ferdinando Anichini, said that he was going to imitate the croaking of a frog "because all of us who live around Gaiole are nicknamed 'frogs' due to the large number of them to be found along the banks of the Masellane."

However, his attempted imitation did not go as he planned, and Corrado said it was impossible to recognise it as the croaking of a frog. Unabashed, the contestant defended himself saying: "Our frogs sound like that because they drink Chianti..." After having said the name 'Chianti' four times on national television – in an era when such types of indirect product promotion were still unknown – Ferdinando went home with a total of 200,000 lire, using the prize money to raise this frog statue.

The astonishing sculpture of the frog gulping down wine and spewing forth water is the work of the Siena-born sculptor Plinio Tammaro. Every year, San Sano now has a week of cultural and artistic events that goes under the title of *La Rana d'Oro* [The Golden Frog].

SIGHTS NEARBY:

THE LUCA CAVA OF SAN GUSMÉ

Giardini Silvio Gigli. Via degli Etruschi. San Gusmè
53019 Castelnuovo Berardenga (SI)

The Luca Cava is a terracotta statue of a man squatting to relieve himself. A strategically-placed hat conceals the front of his anatomy... but not the jet of water that sprays from it. To the left of the niche containing the statue, a stone plaque presents the *Luca Cava* in these terns: "King, emperor, pope, philosopher, poet, workman, peasant, mankind in all his daily affairs. Do not laugh, look at yourself."

The idea for the Luca came to the local landowner Giovanni Bonechi in 1888. In order to accumulate natural fertiliser for his fields, he simply invented a small open-air toilet... Above it he placed this explicit statue with the inscription "Luca Cava, 1888." Taken down in the 1930s for reasons that are not known to us, the statue was installed in its present place in 1972.

Each year during the last week in August and the first two weeks of September the town now holds a *Festa del Luca*, during which a statuette of the *Luca Cava* is awarded to a show-business personality. The idea for such an award originated with the famous journalist and television presenter Silvio Gigli (1910-1988), who was born in Siena. The San Gusmè festival also involves a conference dedicated to the theme of the rural landscape and the preservation of rural traditions.

THE CORONATION OF THE VIRGIN ❽

Church of San Pietro in Badia a Roti
• Open during Sunday mass, 10.00-11.15
• Otherwise, phone: Camilla Sawicki on 338 592 99 12; Claudio Bressan on 339 244 70 23; or Andrea Agresti on 340 543 61 69

A forgotten masterpiece

Hidden away in the Tuscan countryside, to the south-east of Chianti, the church of San Pietro in Badia contains a small masterpiece, unknown even to many of the local residents. Painted in 1472 by Neri di Bicci (1419-1491), this Coronation of the Virgin stands just behind the high altar. Perfectly lit, it is guaranteed to take your breath away when you enter the church. The decorative richness, dazzling palette, and gilt background of the work make this painting a gem which you definitely must not miss if you are in the neighbourhood. Note also its unusual ring of angels around the Virgin.

Commissioned for the church in 1471 by the local parish priest, Father Bartolomeo, the painting was on loan to Florence in the years 1862-1913: the church was undergoing restoration and it was feared the painting might be damaged. The somewhat less successful lunette above the picture depicts The Annunciation.

Built in the 12th century, the church itself was originally part of an abbey, which is now undergoing restoration. Unusually, it is not aligned east-west, which suggests it was built on the site of an earlier structure that dated from pre-Christian times.

PARCO ARTISTICO BUM BUM GÀ

❾

Borrolungo District
Via Ossaia
52025 Montevarchi (AR)
Sculptor: Carmelo Librizzi
• E-Mail : librizzi3@librizzicarmelo.191.it
• Tel: 055 91 02 157 - 329 98 18 574
• Opening hours: daily 9.00-18.00
• Free admission
• Directions: the Borrolungo district which is the site of the Parco Artistico Bum Bum Gà stands about one kilometre from the village, on the other side of the railway track. The way is indicated by various signposts which lead you onto a narrow earthen track. Don't worry: just when you think you have gone the wrong way, you are practically there.

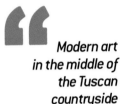

Modern art in the middle of the Tuscan countryside

Created from 1976 onwards by the sculptor and musician Carmelo Librizzi, this Art Park can be visited as an open-air exhibition of works laid out in the beautiful countryside of the Valdarno. However, when you look more closely, you see that there is nothing casual about the way the artist has organised the works. The park is, in effect, a reflection upon the modern art of its day (it was started in the 1970s) and upon how art might develop in the future. Its name is taken from that of the isolated Australian village which is the setting of Luigi Zampa's 1971 film Bello Onesto Emigrato Australia sposerebbe compaesana illibata (Good-looking and honest emigrant to Australia looking for a virgin from his home town with a view to marriage), which starred Alberta Sordi as an Italian provincial rather ill-at-ease in his new world.

Though you might not entirely understand what the park's creator is trying to communicate, a visit to the place is both unusual and pleasant; the location itself is splendid, partly because it is nothing like the typical setting for a display of modern art.

In summer, Carmelo Librizzi organises shows, concerts and events, at which the children from the schools of Montevarchi are more likely to be participants than mere spectators.

THE GOLDEN TREE
IN THE MUNICIPAL MUSEUM OF LUCIGNANO

⑩

22, Piazza del Tribunale
52046 Lucignano (AR)
• Tel: 0575 83 68 99
• E-Mail: lucignano@comune.lucignano.ar.it • http://www.comune.lucignano.ar.it
• Opening hours: in winter, Tuesday, Thursday and Friday 10.00-13.00 and 14.30-
17.30, Saturday and Sunday 10.00-13.00 and 14.30-18.00; in summer: Tuesday,
Wednesday, Thursday, Saturday and Sunday 10.00-13.00 and 14.30-18.00.
Closed on Mondays
• Admission: 3 €, reduced: 2 €.

A Golden Tree that brings good luck to lovers

An exceptional example of the skill of Arezzo's goldsmiths, this Golden Tree has no equal anywhere in the world and is the pride of the Lucignano Municipal Museum. Also known as the "Tree of Life," the "Tree of Lucignano," the "Tree of Love," or the "Tree of St. Francis," this Golden Tree is, in fact, a reliquary. Standing 2.6 m high and made of silver and gilded copper, it was created over the period 1350 to 1471. Ugolino da Vieri and Gabriello d'Antonio are both mentioned as having played a part in its making.

The tree consists of a trunk and twelve branches. At the top is a crucifix and a pelican; the bird was supposed to peck its breast in order to feed its young with its own blood, and thus became a symbol of Christ's sacrifice on the Cross. On the branches – six to each side – are golden leaves, miniatures, enamels, medallions adorned with rock crystal and coral (the latter's colour recalling that of Christ's blood) and small reliquaries that once held fragments of the True Cross (now empty).

The tree was stolen on 28 September 1914. Three years later it was found hidden in a cave outside the village of Sarterano (near Siena), about 60 kilometres to the south of here; however, some of its enamel works and coral pieces were missing; originally there were 72. The name "Tree of Love" comes from the fact that the tree is supposed to bring good luck to the newly-weds – and renewed sexual vigour to the elderly couples – who place flowers or petals at its base.

SIGHTS NEARBY:

THE TRIUMPH OF DEATH

⑪

Church of San Francesco. Piazza San Francesco. 52046 Lucignano (AR)
Built in the 13th century, the church of San Francesco contains a very striking fresco by Bartolo di Fredi (1330-1410), which has recently undergone painstaking restoration. This depicts *The Triumph of Death* with the sort of breath-taking realism that one more readily associates with a modern film poster. In a programme broadcast on RAI3 in 2006, Philippe Daverio described the work as the "first 'period' example of 'comic book art.'"

ROMAN MOSAIC IN THE DE MUNARI CHEMIST'S SHOP

❷

82, Corso Matteoti
53041 Asciano (SI)
• Tel : 0577 71 81 24
• Visits: apply to the chemist. No more than two people at a time. Groups not admitted.
• Shop opening hours: 9.00-13.00 and 15.30-19.30, Saturday 9.00-13.00.

Mosaics to order

A large area of the floor in the back shop of the De Munari pharmacy (formerly Francini Naldi) is part of a Roman mosaic that is said to date from the 1st century AD.

To see this amazing hidden gem, you have to go through the labyrinthine storage area behind the main shop and then descend into the basement. Covering a total of 180 m2, the sumptuous underground pavement was discovered in 1889. The richness and refinement of the mosaic suggested that it was part of thermal baths fed by the sulphurous waters of the Bestina torrent. However, studies by some archaeologists seem to support the notion that it belonged to a villa built by Domitius Afrus, a famous orator from in Nimes in Gaul who served the emperor Caligula (12-41 AD). It is said that afterwards the villa became the property of Domitia Lucilla, the mother of the emperor Marcus Aurelius (121-180 AD).

The chemist is kind enough to allow the curious to see this marvellous feature of his premises. Do not ask to see it when the shop is full or turn up just before closing time. Note: the mosaics were being repaired during my last visit, and this work may still be underwayso perhaps they are still undergoing repair.

THE *ARBORARIO* OF SOUTH TUSCANY **⓭**

Consultation only by appointment with the authors
Contact: annibale1946@yahoo.it
53024 Montalcino (SI)

> *A special library devoted solely to the trees of southern Tuscany*

Known by the untranslatable name of an Arborario, this amazing library dedicated to the trees of southern Tuscany is the very original creation of the naturalist Mario Morellini and the publisher and wine-grower Annibale Parisi.

Each volume is cut in the wood of the tree concerned and measures some 40 by 30 cm and is 12 cm thick. The books are edged with the corresponding bark and within the covering page, decorated with the tree's leaves, one finds a series of compartments containing the fruit and pollen of the tree; samples of its wood, foliage and sap; the parasites that might live within it; and a monograph complete with descriptions and various notes.

The whole scheme has been executed wonderfully, with each volume being a small masterpiece that fully demonstrates the passion and talent of those who devised the project. In effect, this is a library that enables one not only to learn about the plant world but also to touch and smell it. The collection has yet to find a permanent home, but it can be consulted upon application to Annibale Parisi, who acts as its present custodian (see above e-mail address).

Parisi has also set up a small publishing company which produces hand-printed limited-edition facsimiles of books on the history of Montalcino which have long been out of print. In his workshop he also makes pipes, which are not for sale; he himself is not a smoker, but he makes them to offer as gifts. Finally, Annibale is also a wine-grower, and though his Montalcino red wine will not officially be recognised as "Brunello" until 2010, it is still a very pleasant drink. To sample or purchase the wine, make an appointment with the wine cellar at the above-mentioned e-mail address.

THE GIANT SUNDIAL OF PIENZA

⓮

Cathedral of Santa Maria Assunta
Piazza Pio II
53026 Pienza (SI)

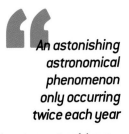

An astonishing astronomical phenomenon only occurring twice each year

The cathedral of Santa Maria Assunta was inaugurated on 29 August 1462. It is remarkable because twice each year the shadow which falls within the nine paving slabs of the area alongside it is exactly the same size as the building itself. A ring carved into the stone corresponds perfectly with the oculus of the cathedral, demonstrating that the correspondence is no matter of chance.

The cathedral was the work of the architect Bernardo Rossellino and was commissioned by Pope Pius II, a native of this town (which later took its name from this famous son). Probably the pontiff wanted an edifice that would make a real impact upon the local population and this is why the architect gave the cathedral a north-south – rather than the usual east-west – alignment. This meant that twice a year the remarkable phenomenon occurred: ten or eleven days after the Spring equinox (on 1 April) and ten or eleven days before the Autumn equinox (on 11 September). The effect was calculated to occur at solar noon, which means one must now allow for the difference between summer and winter time and the gap in minutes between local time as reckoned in the 15th century and current 21st century standard time.

It should be noted that an approximate version of the phenomenon occurs in the days preceding and following the above dates, given that the building's shadow only shifts some 15cm a day.

The extraordinary feature of this cathedral-sundial was only recently rediscovered, thanks to the architect Jan Pieper. To know more, see his *Pienza. Il Progetto di una Visione Umanistica del Mondo*, published by Edizioni Menges in 2000.

THE JULIAN CALENDAR: WHY DID SAINT TERESA OF AVILA DIE ON THE NIGHT BETWEEN 4 AND 15 OCTOBER 1582...?

The Julian calendar – which owes its name to the fact it was instituted during the reign of Julius Caesar – remained in force until the year 1582, when Pope Gregory XIII introduced what became known as the Gregorian calendar. This reform largely concerned the question of leap years; the previous system had resulted in the calendar date lagging behind the actual annual cycle. The most spectacular effect of the introduction of the new calendar was the suppression of ten days in the year 1582. That is why St. Teresa of Avila died on the night between 4 and 15 October 1582...

---

* Étymologiquement, « orienté à l'est » est un pléonasme car « orienté » vient du latin « oriens » : qui se lève. On devrait donc dire d'une église dont le chœur pointe à l'est qu'elle est tout simplement orientée.

PISA

A CATHEDRAL AS A SUNDIAL

Piazza dei Miracoli

❶

O nce a year, on 25 March, Pisa Cathedral is transformed into one immense solar clock, the light filtering through the building serving to announce the advent of the New Year. Before 1749, when the Grand Duke of Tuscany imposed 1 January as the start of the new year, it was traditional for the

> **When the Pisan New Year was celebrated on 25 March**

year to change on 25 March, which fell very close to the spring equinox. On that day the rays of the sun enter the cathedral through an oculus in the main nave and strike a plaque resting on a marble egg. This event is celebrated with a traditional procession and a brief ceremony which ends at midday with the recital of this ritual phrase: "We call upon the intercession of the Blessed Virgin Mary and of St. Ranieri, our patron saint, as, to the greater glory of God, we celebrate the year…." (the number of the Pisan year is in fact one higher than that of the usual calendar).

Reintroduced in the 1980s, this ceremony is also an act of veneration to the Virgin, to whom the cathedral is dedicated. March 25 is, in fact, the Feast of the Annunciation.

SIGHTS NEARBY:

MARK OF THE DEVIL IN PISA CATHEDRAL

❷

The fifth column to your left as you walk down the nave of the cathedral from the main entrance is marked by regular series of holes forming a straight vertical line. Legend has it that these were made by the Devil, who wanted to play his own shady part in the building of the church. The story goes that, like the Devil, the holes are deceitful, for it is almost impossible to count up or down the line without getting confused and coming up with a different sum total each time (see the story concerning the bees of Ferdinando I in Florence, page 48).

AMPHORA FROM THE MARRIAGE FEAST AT CANA

❸

Pisa Cathedral

To the right of the cathedral apse is a column bearing a red porphyry amphora which, according to tradition, was one of those containing the water which Jesus changed into wine at the Marriage Feast of Cana. An inscription records that the precious relic was supposedly brought back from the Holy Land after the First Crusade (1096-1099). In all of the cathedral inventories, the amphora is referred to as the "Epiphany Urn." In fact, the miracle of the changing of water into wine was traditionally believed to have taken place on the Feast of the Epiphany (January 6).

One should point out that other sources say the urn dates from the 4th century AD.

RELIC OF THE CROWN OF THORNS IN THE CHURCH OF SANTA CHIARA

❹

Church of Santa Chiara dall'Opera dell'Ospedale. 67,Via Roma. 56126 Pisa (PI)
The church of Santa Chiara is actually located within the Santa Chiara hospital complex (Azienda Ospedaliera Pisana), at the end of Via Roma, a short walk from Piazza dei Miracoli.

Still green...!

Contrary to what one would expect, the precious relic of Christ's Crown of Thorns that gives its name to Santa Maria della Spina [spina = thorn] is no longer within that church. In fact, Santa Maria della Spina originally stood on the banks of the Arno but - in order to protect it from flooding - in 1871 it was dismantled stone by stone and then rebuilt on its present site. During this "removal," the relic of Christ's Crown of Thorns was moved to Santa Chiara and has stayed there ever since; the tabernacle for the relic which Stagio Stani created in 1534 for the church of Santa Maria della Spina stands empty.

The relic comprises a twisted section of thorn with one long prickle and two smaller ones. It is said to have been brought to the city by a Pisan merchant in 1266 and then presented to the Oratory of Santa Maria al Ponte Novo in 1333. Whilst the famous Crown of Thorns itself was bought by the sainted French King Louis IX in 1239 (see below), it would seem that over the course of the centuries a certain number of thorns were removed from it and presented to various cities as exceptional tokens of gratitude. Thus, Pisa, Rome, Vicenza, and Vasto all received a part of the famous relic.

THE CROWN OF THORNS

After the Holy Shroud of Turin, the Crown of Thorns is considered the most important relic of Christ's Passion.

The first reference to the survival of the relic dates from 409, when St. Paulinus of Nola mentions it amongst the relics to be found in the Basilica of Mount Zion in Jerusalem. Moved to Byzantium in order to prevent it falling into the hands of the Persians, the Crown of Thorns was subsequently sold to the Venetians in 1238 by the Latin emperor Baudouin de Courtenay, whose Crusader realm was facing serious economic difficulties. St. Louis (1215-1270) bought in 1239 and then had a befitting reliquary built to house it: the Sainte Chapelle in Paris (some of the stained glass windows in the church record this event). After the French Revolution, the relics were entrusted to the canons of the Chapter of Notre-Dame in Paris, and they are still to be found in that cathedral, where the Crown of Thorns is put on display for the faithful once a year (see *Secret Paris* by the same publisher).

The authenticity of such relics is, of course, difficult to establish. However, on the one known occasion when the present reliquary was opened (1940), it was discovered that the leaves had dried but the ring of plaited thorns was still green!

WIND ROSE IN PIAZZA DEI MIRACOLI

Piazza dei Miracoli

❺

Names of the winds

Above the roof of the ticket office in Piazza dei Miracoli is an elegant wind rose surmounted by an arch and a capital. It gives the direction of the prevailing winds. From the top clockwise, the main winds in the Mediterranean are indicated as follows (winds are named after the direction from which they blow):

Mezz: the *mezzogiorno or ostro,* the south wind
Libe: the *libeccio*, the south-west wind
Pon: the *ponente*, the west wind
Maes: the *maestrale*, the north-west wind
Tram: the *tramontana*, the north wind
Grec: the *grecale*, the north-east wind
Lev: the *levante*, the east wind
Scir: the *scirocco*, the south-east wind

On the pediment of the charterhouse at Calci near Pisa an identical rose wind is positioned rather differently: the east is shown at the top, in accordance with the medieval custom of placing the direction of Jerusalem above all others.

SIGHTS NEARBY:

PENNON FROM THE TURKISH FLAGSHIP AT THE BATTLE OF LEPANTO

❻

Church of Santo Stefano dei Cavalieri
Piazza dei Cavalieri
Opening hours: daily 9.30-20.00. Admission: 1.50 €.

Standing in a vast monumental square to which it gives it name, the church of Santo Stefano dei Cavalieri was built in 1569; its facade was completed some 40 years later. This was the place of worship of the Knights of Santo Stefano, whose palace also stood in this square. This military order was responsible for combating the pirates who infested the Mediterranean, seizing ships and raiding coastal settlements.

The interior of the church is largely decorated with the pennons and fanions taken from the pirate ships captured or sunk by the Order. The most prestigious of these trophies is, however, the standard of the Turkish flagship at the battle of Lepanto. This is often referred to as a flamme because of its flame-like shape.

In Piazza dei Cavalieri, the Palazzo del Consiglio dell'Ordine di Santo Stefano is surmounted by an inscription which begins *Ferdinando Magno Duce Etruriae S.P.Q.P...* Note how the Grand Duke of Tuscany adapted the famous SPQR *(Senatus Populus Que Romanus)*, to become SPQP: the Pisan Senate and People.

OLD FOUNDLINGS HOSPITAL ❼

Library and Documentary Archive of the Pisan Hospitals
108, Via Santa Maria
• Opening hours: Monday to Thursday 8.00-13.00 and 15.00-17.00, Friday 8.00-13.00.
56 and 60, Via Santa Maria
12, Via dell'Occhio

Just a short walk from Piazza dei Miracoli is the old Foundlings Hospital. Right above the doorway is a touching reminder of the building's past: a sculpture of a baby wrapped in swaddling.

Where children could be abandoned discreetly

In fact, right up to 1921 it was possible to abandon unwanted infants here…

The process was facilitated by something called a "wheel," a sort of rotating cradle: the infant was placed on the outside section and then the table was rotated so that, no questions asked, it was moved inside. The contraption still exists, only now it is inside the building: just push open the door at the opening times given above and you can see it.

There are similar haut-reliefs elsewhere in the city indicating other places that received abandoned children – for example, at numbers 56 and 60 Via Santa Maria, which were once 9 and 10 of the old Via Santa Maria de Ponte Novo, a street which used to ran down to the Ponte Novo (this bridge over the Arno was destroyed in the 19th century). Another, rather crude, depiction of an infant can be seen set into the wall of no. 12 Via dell'Occhio.

THE FOUNDLINGS' WHEEL

It is said that in 787, Dateus, a priest in Milan, began placing a large basket outside his church so that abandoned infants could be left there. More organised initiatives for the reception of abandoned children were begun by the Hospice des Chanoines in Marseilles from 1188 onwards, with Pope Innocent III (1198-1216) later giving the practice the Church's benediction; he had been horrified by the terrible sight of the bodies of abandoned infants floating in the Tiber and was determined to do something to save them. So the doors of convents were equipped with a sort of rotating cradle which made it possible for parents to leave their infant anonymously and without exposing them to the elements. The infant was left in the outside section of the cradle, and then the parent rang a bell so that the nuns could activate the mechanism and bring the child inside. Access to the "turntable" was, however, protected by a grill so narrow that only newborn infants would fit through… Abandoned during the 19th century, the system has, over the last twenty years, had to be re-adopted at various places in Europe due to the sharp upturn in the number of infants abandoned.

WHY IS THE CROSS OF THE ORDER OF SANTO STEFANO SO SIMILAR TO THE MALTESE CROSS?

For the laymen there is very little difference between the Cross of the Military Order of Santo Stefano and the more famous Cross of the Knights of Malta. The two colours – red and white – are the opposite way round, but the form of the cross is identical. Founded in 1561, the Military Order of Santo Stefano was intended to promote the Christian faith, defend the Mediterranean against pirates, and free Christian slaves. It first fought alongside the Order of St. John of Jerusalem in the defence of Malta, the island which would give the latter order its more familiar title. As a symbol of the bond between them, the knights of Santo Stefano took the same cross as their symbol; however, like the Knights Templar (who had disappeared from western history in 1307), they chose the colour of the blood of Christ for the cross itself. Founded in 11th century Jerusalem by merchants from Amalfi (near Naples), the Sovereign Order of the Knights Hospitaller of St. John of Jeruslam (the future Knights of Malta) first took as their symbol that of the port of Amalfi, merely dropping the blue background. Then, in 1130, Raymond de Puy transformed the charitable brotherhood into a military Order and obtained from Pope Innocent II the right to a white cruciform emblem; the colour was chosen to avoid confusion with the red cross of the Templars. Shortly after being driven off the island of Rhodes by the Turks in 1523, the Order would settle on Malta. At that point, the red flag of the island – inherited from the period when it had been occupied by the Normans – became the background to the white cross. And thus the Maltese Cross came about.

THE MEANING OF THE EIGHT POINTS IN THE MALTESE CROSS AND THE CROSS OF THE ORDER OF SANTO STEFANO

The eight points in the Maltese Cross signify various things:

- the eight nationalities of the original knights of the Order of St. John of Jerusalem (the future Order of Malta) or the eight principles they undertook to live by: spirituality, simplicity, humility, compassion, justice, pity, sincerity and patience.

- the eight virtues which a knight of the Order of Malta was expected to possess: loyalty, pity, frankness, courage, honour, contempt of death, solidarity with the sick and poor, respect for the Catholic Church.

- the Eight Beatitudes which Christ listed in his Sermon on the Mount (St. Matthew's Gospel, Chapter 5):

Blessed are the poor in spirit: for theirs is the kingdom of heaven. (Verse 3)

Blessed are the meek: for they shall posses the land. (Verse 4)

Blessed are they who mourn: for they shall be comforted. (Verse 5)

Blessed are they that hunger and thirst after justice: for they shall have their fill. (Verse 6)

Blessed are the merciful: for they shall obtain mercy. (Verse 7)

Blessed are the clean of heart: for they shall see God. (Verse 8)

Blessed are the peacemakers: for they shall be called the children of God. (Verse 9)

Blessed are they that suffer persecution for justice' sake, for theirs is the kingdom of heaven. (Verse 10)

THE MUSSOLINI STAINED GLASS PORTRAIT IN THE CHURCH OF SAN FRANCESCO

❽

Piazza San Francesco. 56127 Pisa (PI)

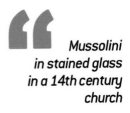

Mussolini in stained glass in a 14th century church

In the 1930s Francesco Mossmeyer was commissioned to carry out restoration work on the church of San Francesco. He produced new stained glass windows for the left side of the nave. Naturally these depict episodes from the lives of the saints… but there is also a figure who bears a striking resemblance to Benito Mussolini. The windows were produced when Il Duce ruled supreme in Italy, so some have argued that this similarity is far from being an accident…

ANOTHER SOUVENIR FROM THE MUSSOLINI ERA

From the top of the famous Leaning Tower, looking towards the Baptistery, one can see a rather curiously-shaped building directly outside the city walls. This Istituto Technico Industriale was built during the period of Fascism and its M-shaped design was clearly intended as a homage to Mussolini

WHY SAINT-TROPEZ OWES ITS NAME TO A PISAN KNIGHT...

In the year 68 AD, the Roman emperor Nero was present at a ceremony in the Temple of Diana at Pisa and claimed "Diana is mistress of the world." Torpè, a convert to Christianity, dared to contradict him: "You are mistaken, Nero. There is only one master; and that master is God!"

Upon leaving Pisa, Nero asked a certain Satellicus to make sure, by whatever means necessary, that Torpè abjured his faith. Tied to a column, Torpè was flogged; but at the very first strokes, the column collapsed on the torturers and upon the said Satellicus. Then the Christian was stretched out on the wheel, but that, too, broke. Then he was thrown to savage beasts, but they apparently had no appetite for him. Eventually he was beheaded and his body — together with a cockerel and a dog — was put in a skiff and pushed out into the Arno.

As you might have gathered, this boat finally ran aground at Saint-Tropez, which took Torpè as its patron saint.

Cogolin, a nearby village, takes its name from the coq on the boat, and Grimaud, another nearby village, from its canine companion (*grimaud* in Old French meant "dog").

The church of San Torpè.

20, Via Carlo Fedeli.

Open weekdays 9.00-12.00 and 15.45-17.30,

Sunday and holidays 15.45- 17.30.

THE CHAPTER ROOM OF SAINT BONAVENTURE

Cercle A.C.L.I. San Francesco
Piazza San Francesco

❾

• Opening hours: Tuesday to Saturday 16.00-19.00, Sunday 9.30-13.00 and 14.30-19.00.
• Access is reserved to club members, but one may take a stroll here after asking for the keys.
• Reservation the day before (evenings) at the home number of Gabriella: 050 57 27 45.

An unknown gem

iving onto the left side of the cloister of the church of San Francesco, the monks' magnificent Chapter Room is decorated with frescoes by Taddeo di Bartolo (1362-1422). Tradition has it that it was in this room that St. Bonaventure held the meeting which, in 1263, instituted the practice of ringing bells at nightfall – a custom which would ultimately result in the prayer of the Angelus. This totally unknown place can be visited upon asking for the keys at the San Francesco branch of the ACLI (Italian Catholic Workers Association), whose premises adjoin the cloister. It is advisable to contact Gabriella, the club's permanent secretary, the day before.

WHY IS THERE NO BUILDING AT NO. 19, LUNGARNO GALILEI?

The second chapel on the right behind the choir in the church of San Francesco contains the tomb of Ugolino della Gherardesca, together with those of two of his sons and two of his grandsons. Dante himself gives us an account of the terrible end of this very powerful 13th century politician and sea captain. After a meteoric rise, Ugolino would take some ill-advised decisions that resulted in popular discontent and ultimately in uprisings against him. However, it was primarily the fact that he murdered by his own hand the nephew of the archbishop of Pisa which brought about his downfall and terrible death. In 1288 he, his two sons and two grandsons were locked up in what subsequently became known as the *Torre della Fame* [Hunger Tower]; it no longer exists. The key was thrown into the Arno and the five prisoners were left to starve to death.

The bodies of the wretched men were buried in the cloister of the monastery of San Francesco, where they would remain until 1902, when they were transferred to the chapel in the church (a plaque now marks their previous resting-place). Recent DNA analysis has confirmed that these are the bodies of members of three generations of the same family. The *palazzo* of Ugolino della Gherardesca used to stand at 19 Lungoarno Galilei. That street number now corresponds to the only area of open space along the entire city embankments of the Arno: even now the curse of the Gherardesca family discourages property developers.

Tomb of Ugolino della Gherardesca. Chapel of the Conti della Gherardesca. Church of San Francesco. Piazza San Francesco.

THE LAST PILLORY RING IN PIAZZA CAIROLI ❿

Piazza Cairoli

> **Where thieves and other wrongdoers were exposed to public derision**

The thick metal ring at the base of a column in Piazza Cairoli (the one furthest from the river) is a reminder of much crueller days.

It was here that criminals and wrongdoers were chained for public pillory; in fact the square used to be called Piazza della Berlina (*berlina* = pillory). Here, the criminals sentenced to this form of punishment (lasting anything from a few hours to a few days) were left at the mercy of public wrath and derision: they could be insulted, spat upon and even hit. Pillories would be abolished throughout Italy at the end of the 18th century; in Tuscany they came to an end with the abolition of torture (and capital punishment) in 1786.

SIGHTS NEARBY:

AN OLD-STYLE WEIGHTS AND MEASURES CONVERSION TABLE ⓫

15, Piazza delle Vettovaglie
56127 Pisa (PI)

On 28 July 1861 Italy replaced the old units of weight and measure – which could vary from region to region – with the new metric system. It took time for people to learn and accept the new measures, and in the interim conversion tables were displayed in towns and villages throughout the country - primarily in the marketplace or on the main street where market gardeners set up their stalls.

In Pisa, one of these conversion tables can still be seen at number 15 in Piazza Vettovaglie, the old marketplace. To the right of this table, a glass panel in the ground gives you a view down into one of the city's old underground grain silos.

Such conversion tables still survive in a number of other towns, including Campaglia Marittima (outside Livorno), where it can be seen in Via Roma.

PALAZZO ALLA GIORNATA

⑫

43/44, Lungarno Antonio Pacinotti

The extraordinary origin of Palazzo Alla Giornata

Located on the banks of the Arno, Palazzo alla Giornata (meaning "by the day") was built in the 17th century and currently houses the offices of the Chancellor of Pisa University. A bronze plaque on the pediment of the façade is engraved with the name of the palazzo; underneath – at the level of the keystone of the vault – hang three chain links.

Various theories have been put forward with regard to the name and the symbolic significance of the chain. In his *Dizionario Geografico Fisico della Toscana*, Emanuele Repetti admits to being unable to solve the enigma, but does mention that the palazzo is said to have incorporated the church of San Biago alle Catene (*catena* = chain) when it was built. The most likely theory, however, seems to be the following.

In the 17th century, the ship carrying a Pisan knight to Sardinia was boarded by Saracens. After fierce fighting, the knight was taken prisoner and carried off to Algiers, where he was entrusted to the keeping of one of the Bey's favourites. Impressed by the Pisan's courage, the favourite suggested that he should abjure his religion, "take the turban," and enter the service of the Bey. With each refusal from the Italian, his captor made the conditions of his captivity even harsher. One day, seeing that the man continued to respect the Friday fast by abstaining from meat, he mockingly promised: "The Friday when you agree to eat meat, I will give you your freedom." Some months later, the prisoner asked his gaoler for a meal of meat and rich desserts even though it was a Friday. Convinced that this meant the Pisan knight was abjuring his faith, the Arab kept his promise and restored the man's freedom, giving him as a souvenir three links of the chain he had had to wear in captivity.

What he did not know was that, that year, Christmas fell on a Friday, thus Christians were for that one day exempt from the rule of fasting.

Upon his return to Pisa, the knight had this palace built on the banks of the Arno. The three links of the chain were hung as an ex-voto just above the entrance, and the words *alla Giornata* were engraved on the pediment. The phrase was intended to remind people that even in the worst adversity one must maintain hope; one day is enough to bring about a complete turnaround in one's fortunes.

PUBLIC TOILETS OF THE ALBERGO COBIANCHI ⑬

Piazza XX Settembre
• Opening hours: 9.00-13.00 and 15.00-19.00.
• Fee: 0.50 €.

From luxury hotel to public convenience

At the beginning of the 20th century, the boom in tourism meant that new hotels were built in a number of Italian cities. Providing a new service to meet the needs of an increasingly urbanised lifestyle, these specialised in short-stay customers – either tourists passing through or people from the outlying areas who had to stay in town overnight. Work on this particular hotel in Pisa unearthed 700 gold coins bearing the image of the Roman emperor Augustus (for some obscure reason, only 229 are accounted for!), with the building finally being opened to the public in 1926. The disastrous flood of 1966, when the nearby Arno burst its banks, devastated the hotel, which was not restored because changing trends had led to a sharp decline in its clientele. However, some restoration work was carried out in 1998, to convert the place into public toilets. This means the present-day visitor gets the chance to walk down the two long corridors which used to be lined with bedrooms and bathrooms. Despite the damage caused by the flood and subsequent neglect, one still gets some idea of the luxury and refinement of the original establishment, the name of whose owner, Cleopatro Cobianchi, can still be seen on the sign. Cobianchi would also set up various other short-stay hotels, most notably in Milan and Turin.

SANTA BONA: THE PATRON SAINT OF HOTELIERS

Born in 1156 in a modest house of the San Martino district in Pisa, Bona would lose her father, Bernardo, when she was three years old. Her Corsican-born mother, Berta, then struggled against hardship to raise the child. When the girl was 7, she had a vision of receiving a benediction for the crucifix she was passing. This was the first of a number of visions that would lead her to dedicate herself to the religious life. When just 13, Bona set out on a pilgrimage to Jerusalem. Captured by the Saracens during her return voyage, she suffered terribly as their prisoner. Released thanks to a Pisan merchant who "bought" her, she would nevertheless not give up her calling as a pilgrim, dedicating herself to helping those who found themselves in difficulty while travelling along the dangerous pilgrimage routes of the times. She went nine times to Santiago de Compostela (a journey which took around nine months) and on numerous occasions to Rome. She would make her last pilgrimage to Santiago at the age of 48, "transported" there by the apostle himself. On 2 March 1962, Pope John XXIII declared her the patron saint of hoteliers. Thus St. Bona is much venerated by those working in the tourist trade.
Church of San Martino. 1, Piazza San Martino.

THE WELL OF SAINT UBALDESCA

14

Church of San Sepolcro
Piazza San Sepolcro
Mass: Saturday at 18.00.

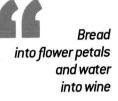

Bread into flower petals and water into wine

The church of San Sepolcro has a well that is associated with a remarkable 12th century miracle.

Born in Calcinia (near Pisa) around 1136, Ubaldesca Taccini would from a very early age reveal her great spirituality and charity. One day, while she was working in the fields, a stranger asked her for a piece of bread. Without hesitating, the girl ran home and filled her smock with food. From a distance, her father saw what she was doing and, when he caught up with her, forbade her to give their food to a stranger. Otherwise what would they have to eat? For the first time in her life Ubaldesca found herself forced to lie, saying that she merely had wild flowers in her smock. A miracle then took place: multicoloured petals fell from the smock, flying off in the breeze.

At 15 years of age Ubaldesca would become a nun within the Hospital of the Knights of St. John of Jerusalem (later the Knights of Malta) which had been built around the church of San Sepolcro in Pisa. Thereafter she would dedicate herself to helping pilgrims.

One day, whilst she was drawing water from the well, a group of pilgrims on their way to Rome asked her for something to drink. She raised the pail from the well, and to everyone's amazement the water had been transformed into wine…

Ubaldesca is the patron saint of Calcinia, her home town, and is venerated by the Order of Malta.

The entrance to the church is a few steps below street level. Like many other buildings in Pisa, the church has subsided because of underground infiltration by the waters of the Arno. (See "The Other Leaning Towers" below).

THE OTHER LEANING TOWERS OF PISA

As well as the famous tower in Piazza dei Miracoli, Pisa has three other bell towers that stand at an angle to the vertical: the 12th century San Michele degli Salzi, in the Orticaria district; San Sisto, near Piazza dei Cavalieri; and San Nicola, in Via Santa Maria. Being incorporated within the surrounding buildings, the latter bell tower appears to be in no danger of falling down. It is unusual in that the base is cylindrical, with the body of the tower then becoming octagonal before ending up hexagonal.

San Sisto - Via dei Mille.
San Michele degli Scalzi - Via San Michele degli Scalzi.
San Nicola - Via Santa Maria.

STATUE OF KINZICA DE SISMONDI

⑮

7, Via San Martino

*Kinzica,
heroine of Pisa:
legend and fact*

Via San Martino, on the left bank of the Arno, stands in an area of the city that was once called Kinzica. Here, there is a curious marble statue of an elegant Roman matron that dates from the 3rd century AD. Over time, the figure depicted became identified with the name of the district itself.

Alhough there are various versions of the story of how a young woman saved the inhabitants of Pisa from Saracen raiders, it does seem the story is based on real events.

In 1004-1005, or 1016 or 1024 – the date varies – the Pisan fleet was besieging Reggio Calabria in order to drive out the Saracens. But the pirates took advantage of the fact that Pisa itself had been left almost undefended and attacked the city. According to one account, Kinzica, who could not sleep that night, raised the alarm by ringing the bell in the Palazzo degli Anziani, thus awakening the people of the city and enabling them to escape… or perhaps arm themselves and drive off the Saracens… or perhaps (according to a third version) the mere sound of the bells scared off the attackers. There is even a version in which Kinzica, first to see the advancing enemy, took up arms against them and distinguished herself by her courage in battle.

Then there is her name itself: some argue it comes from Arabic (the district where the girl lived was that inhabited principally by foreigners), others that it derives from the old Lombard dialect…

One thing is certain: for the people of Pisa, Kinzica is a heroine. She is remembered with particular veneration during the annual *Regatta delle Repubbliche Marittime*, a boating competition between the four great maritime republics of Italy: Pisa, Venice, Amalfi and Genoa. The event is hosted by each of these four cities in turn.

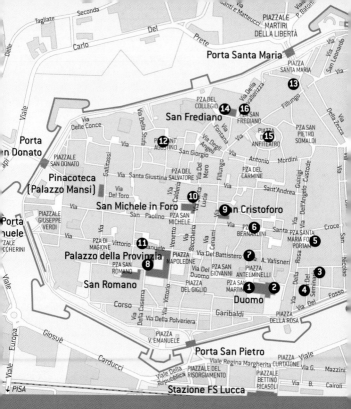

LUCCA

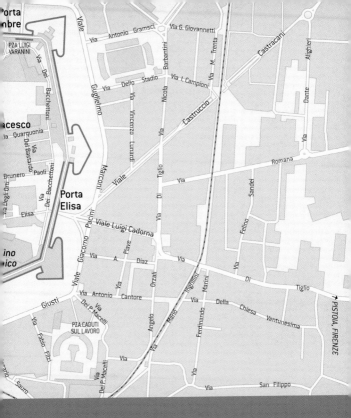

SISTE MIRVM AD MIRARE PRODIGIV
A D M CCCXXXIV
AB SERVV HVIVS FILIO IOANNIS
... ATA K TENSIS PRESBVS
APVD ARD SECVTIL IN SVI NECEM
...

ALMÆ CRVCIS ARAM DEVOTE VISITANTIBVS
CVM PIA OBLATIONE ET ALTARIS OSCVLO
DATVR REMISSIO PECCATORVM.

HOC ALTARE PRIVILEGIATVM IN PERPETVV
EXISTIT PRO SACERDOTIBVS EIVS
ECCLESIÆ, EX CONCESSIONE SANCTISS
D.D. ALEXANDRI PP. VII SVB DATVM ROMA
DIE VI X BRIS   M DC LVII

UNUSUAL EX-VOTOS IN THE CATHEDRAL OF SAN MARTINO

❶

Piazza San Martino
55100 Lucca (LU)

A metal axe that suddenly went soft

On a pillar just in front of the Chapel of the Holy Visage in the Cathedral of San Martino is a strange axe sticking through a thick grill. Above, a Latin inscription records a miracle that happened in 1334, when a certain Giovanni di Lorenzo from the Comté d'Arras in France tried to help a man who had been attacked in the town of Pietralunga (Umbria). The victim died of his wounds and, as they had not witnessed the attack, the townspeople assumed that the Frenchman was the murderer. Imprisoned and then sentenced to be beheaded, he prayed to the Holy Visage of Lucca (see below) for the truth to come to light. When the executioner brought his iron axe down on Giovanni's neck, the blade suddenly went so soft that it did not even leave a mark on the skin. The miracle was repeated another two times before finally, in accordance with custom, the condemned man was set free and his innocence recognised.

An ill-lit glass case not far from this axe in the church contains a real horse's tail. This unusual trophy was offered as an ex-voto to the Holy Visage (see below) by Stefano Orsetti, a native of Lucca who served as the commanding officer of a cavalry regiment in the Austro-Hungarian army; he had cut the tail from the horse of an enemy during a battle against the Turks fought at Petrovaradin (Hungary).

THE MIRACLE OF THE HOLY VISAGE

The "Holy Visage" is a famous wooden crucifix which is said to bear an actual likeness of Christ. The legend goes that after Joseph of Arimathea and Nicodemus had lowered Christ's body from the Cross, Nicodemus - who naturally remembered what Christ had looked like in life – was made responsible for recording the scene as faithfully as possible. Having no talent himself as a sculptor, he would however find the following morning he nevertheless discovered that a crucifix had been miraculously carved by an unknown hand. Hidden in a safe place when Nicodemus died, the crucifix was brought to Christian Europe some six centuries later by Bishop Gualfredo, acting at the behest of an angel. The ship carrying the relic docked at the town of Luni in Liguria, whose inhabitants wished to keep the precious object for themselves. However, the two oxen drawing the cart with the crucifix would, of their own volition, take the road for Lucca. The Holy Visage is now to be seen in a small chapel within the Cathedral of San Martino, and it is venerated each 13 September during the course of a special procession, *La Luminara*.

HIC MEM
CRETICVS
EPI DEDI
V REST
LA DENIVE
MAR FICV
NVLLV
S VADE
E OVIV
OM FV
INTVS
NH IES
VS GRA
S NEN
E TAN
NE M

+ SEPVLTVRA ROLLANDI
DEBRICA IV +

THE LABYRINTH IN LUCCA CATHEDRAL

❷

Piazza San Martino. 55100 Lucca (LU)

Carved to the right of the main doorway into the Cathedral is a labyrinth measuring some 50 cm in diameter. The accompanying Latin inscription reads: "This is the labyrinth designed by the Cretan Daedalus. None of those who ventured into it ever found their way out, with the exception of Theseus, who did so thanks to the thread Ariadne gave him out of love." Various explanations have been put forward regarding the symbolic significance of the labyrinth (see below). This one was once the last hope of salvation for those sentenced to death. On his way to the scaffold, the condemned man was brought to the labyrinth, and if he could, at his first attempt, trace a route through it, then his life was spared.

LABYRINTHS

According to legend, one of the first ever labyrinths was constructed by Daedalus to contain the Minotaur, a monster born of the love of Queen Pasiphae, wife of Minos, King of Crete, for a bull. Archaeologists have argued that the elaborate ground plan of Minos's royal palace at Knossos (Crete) was the origin of this legend. Only three people were said to have found their way through this mythical labyrinth. One was Theseus, who had come to Crete to kill the monster; he was helped in his task by Ariadne, Minos's daughter, who had fallen in love with him and gave him a thread so that he could find his way back out (the famous "Ariadne's thread"). The other two were Daedalus himself and his son Icarus, after Minos had imprisoned them there. Some legends say the king was anxious that the secret of the labyrinth should never be betrayed; others claim the imprisonment was punishment for having given Ariadne the idea of the thread. The labyrinth was so perfectly designed that even Daedalus could only find his way out by flying above it, having made himself and his son wings out of feathers and wax. Designs or engravings of labyrinths are to be found in numerous ancient civilisations (Mesopotamian, Egyptian, Hopi, Navajo, etc.) and there are vestiges in Europe dating back to prehistoric times. The symbol of the labyrinth was also used by early Christianity and can be seen in the Rome catacombs, as well as Italian churches such as San Michele Maggiore (Pavia) and the cathedral in Lucca. There was also a mosaic in San Savino (Piacenza). In France there are fine examples in the cathedrals of Chartres and Rheims. Usually these are located on the western side of the church, the direction associated with demons and death because it is in the west that the sun sets. As it was believed that demons could only move in straight lines, the elaborate path of the labyrinth prevented them reaching the altar. The labyrinth is also associated with ideas regarding the course of life, reflecting the notion that Man is lost within the Universe and does not know where he comes from or where he is going. But the very centre of the labyrinth, reached after an often painful and tortuous journey of initiation, might well represent a point of divine salvation, a heavenly Jerusalem. The flight of Daedalus and Icarus to arrive at this goal therefore symbolises the elevation of the spirit towards knowledge and of the soul towards God. Similarly, the thread with which Adriane supplies Theseus shows how the love of one person for another can provide another way out of the absurdity of the human condition.

VISIT TO THE HOUSE OF SAINT GEMMA GALGANI ❸

Congregazione Missionaria Sorelle di S. Gemma. Casa Giannini
10, Via del Seminario. 55100 Lucca (LU)
• Visits by appointment only.
• Opening hours; summer, 9.00-12.30 and 15.00-19.00; winter, 9.00-12.00 and
15.00-18.00 • Free admission and guided tour
• Tel/Fax: 0583 48 237 • E-Mail: cgianninilucca@libero.it

A forgotten saint

Venerated rather more in Spain and Chile than in Italy, St. Gemma Galgani (see below) lived in Lucca at 10, Via del Seminario. The congregation responsible for the chapel of Santa Maria della Rosa (see page 181) also provides visitors with an interesting and moving guided tour through her house. The visit begins in the dining-room, which has been kept as it was at the time of the saint's death. A plaque on the table indicates where she sat at meals. The rooms are adorned with photographs and a powerfully expressive crucifix, which is contained within a cabinet that can be kept open or shut. Most astonishing of all is the photograph of the saint which reveals how exceptionally beautiful she was. The relics relating to her stigmata are particularly interesting. There are pieces of cloth from her garments that are stained with the blood that flowed from her wounds and from her crown of thorns. There is also the copy of her autobiography which the devil tried to burn…

SAINT GEMMA GALGANI

Born on 12 March 1878 at Camigliano (outside Lucca), where her parents kept a chemist's shop, Gemma Galgani dedicated her life to the love of Jesus, whose stigmata she bore. She was admitted to the care of the Passionist Fathers, who took not only the three vows of chastity, poverty and obedience, but also a fourth one that committed them to propagateveneration of Christ's Passion. She died in great pain on Easter Saturday, 11 April 1903, and was canonised in 1940.

STIGMATA

The stigmata are traces in the hands, feet and side of the wounds that Christ suffered during his Passion and Crucifixion. The phenomenon is still the subject of debate, but there are various famous cases of the unexplained appearance of such lesions.

The most famous case is obviously that of St. Francis of Assisi, who in 1224 had a vision of a six-winged seraph hovering in the air before him while he was nailed to a cross just as Christ had been. After that vision came to an end, St. Francis became aware of the marks on his own hands and feet. Other famous cases include those of St. Catherine of Siena, St. John of God, Padre Pio (1918-1968), Marthe Robin and St. Gemma Galgani. Brother Elie in the Umbrian monastery of Calvi (not far from Rome) is said to bear the marks of the stigmata ever year during the period of Lent.

ROMAN WALL IN THE CHURCH ❹
OF SANTA MARIA DELLA ROSA

Via della Rosa - 55100 Lucca (LU)
• Visits by appointment only: contact the Congregazione Missionaria Sorelle di Santa Gemma
Casa Giannini. 10, Via del Seminario - 55100 Lucca (LU).
• Tel/Fax: 0583 48 237
• E-Mail: cgianninilucca@libero.it

Sole remnant of Lucca's Roman walls

L ucca is one of the few cities in Italy to maintain intact its original defensive walls, all 4.2 kilometres of them. Built in the 16th and 17th centuries, these Renaissance fortifications now provide the inhabitants with a very pleasant place to stroll and take the air.

Before these ramparts were built, the city had walls dating from the Middle Ages and from Roman times; traces of these still exist, even if they are much less easy to identify.

Among the various remnants of the medieval citywalls (the plural is doubly correct because the fortifications developed over the course of time) are two particularly spectacular city gates: the Porta San Gervasio e Protasio that stands at the corner of Via Santa Croce and Via dei Fossi, and the Porta Borghi, at the end of Via Fillungo.

As for the Roman walls, the local newspapers frequently report that road or building work has unearthed yet more remains of these. However, the only place where an extant section of the walls can be seen by visitors is within the Chapel of Santa Maria della Rosa, in the street of the same name. The Maria della Rosa in question – a Madonna presenting the Christ Child with a rose – appears in a 14th century fresco over the main altar.

The entire left wall of the chapel is part of the old Roman ramparts. Dating from the 2nd century BC, the spectacular wall is made up of opus quadratum – that is, square-cut blocks of stone assembled without mortar. Outside, on the dividing-strip along the street, some blocks of stone have been laid out to indicate the presence of the Roman wall; however, they are not in their original location.

GUIDED TOUR OF LUCCA'S THREE MAIN WALLSLa Giunchiglia - Lucca Tourist Guides 55100 Lucca (LU)
Tel: 0583 341612. E-Mail: lagiunchiglia@tin.it. www.lagiunchiglia.net

---

CARDIO-TREKKING AROUND THE CITY WALLS
The city council of Lucca has recently come up with an original idea that combines a visit to the town walls and an assessment of your fitness. All you have to do is run (or walk) for 12 minutes, then measure the distance covered thanks to the markers fixed in the ground. Using the table based on the Cooper Test (named after the doctor who devised this "fitness barometer") you can then assess what sort of condition you are in. The table is available free of charge from the Main Tourist Office (Piazzale Verdi - Tel: 0583 583150).

THE MERIDIAN IN THE CHURCH OF SANTA MARIA FORIS PORTAM

❺

Piazza Santa Maria Foris Portam
55100 Lucca (LU)

A plaque which tells the time...

In Santa Maria Foris Portam (the name recalls the fact that this 12th/13th century church was built outside the gate in the Roman walls) there is a curious plaque on the last column to the right nearest the choir. The inscription reads:
"Passage to Roman Time:
The Equation of Time + 7 minutes and 55 seconds
Difference calculated by Enrico Pucci in 1875
Engraved in marble by the City Council".
On the floor just below it is a meridian in white marble.

In the past, each Italian town determined the time on the basis of local solar time. Then, in the second half of the 19th century, it was decided that there should be a national measure of time based on the meridian of the capital. Known as "Roman time", this was adopted by Milan in 1866, Turin and Bologna in 1867, Venice in 1880 and Lucca in 1875. However, in adapting to the new hour, a precise measurement was required of the difference between previous local time and the new standard – that is, of the difference in longitude between Rome and the city concerned. This is what is commemorated by this plaque in the church of Santa Maria Foris Portam. Enrico Pucci* calculated that since Lucca and Rome varied in longitude by two degrees – 10° 29'E and 12° 29'E respectively – then the Tuscan city had to add 7 minutes 55 seconds to become synchronised with the Italian capital. In doing so, he must have used the meridian that runs across the floor of the nave just in front of the main altar; unfortunately, this no longer functions as a sundial.

Whilst a national Italian time did serve to coordinate activities within Italy, it did not resolve the problems caused by difference in time standards between neighbouring countries. With the advent of railways, postal services and regular shipping, these time differences became increasingly problematical. A full-scale international solution had to be found. By adopting the principle of time zones, the 1884 Washington Conference would set in place a coherent system that still works today.

THE EQUATION OF TIME

The Equation of Time is the difference between average solar time and real solar time, and can vary during the course of the year. In effect, it is the difference between time as indicated by a sundial and time as given by a clock. This difference is due to the elliptical orbit of the Earth and the inclination of its axis of rotation with respect to the plane of its orbit.

* Enrico Pucci (Lucca 1848 - Florence 1891) was a scientist who specialised in geodesy, the branch of science that determines the exact position of geographical points and studies the shape and size of the Earth.

SIGHTS NEARBY:

THE REBELLIOUS WINDOW JAMB OF PALAZZO BERNARDINI ❻

Located in the square to which it gives its name, Palazzo Bernardini has one very unusual and inexplicable feature: the right jamb of the ground-floor window to the right of the main doorway has curved and come away from the wall. The protruding base of the jamb is, in fact, held in place by a metal bracket designed to prevent it becoming detached from the wall even further. In itself, this would be nothing remarkable, if it were not for the fact that all of the several attempts to repair or replace the stone have been unsuccessful. It is said that when the palazzo was being built in the 16th century, a religious painting that stood at the site of the jamb was destroyed – and that this mysterious deformation of the window is the result of that act of sacrilege.

WHALE PLAQUE ON THE CHURCH OF I SERVI ❼

On the façade of the church of I Servi there is a plaque behind a grill which bears an inscription relating to an unusual episode in the city's history. In 1495 a whale was washed up on the shore nearby and its body was then exhibited for the townsfolk in front of this church. The spectacle was forbidden to children, for fear it would cause them to have nightmares...

THE EAGLE OF CASTRUCCIO CASTRACANI ❽

At the end of the Cortile degli Svizzeri, within the building that houses the administration of the Province of Lucca, the remnants of the fresco of an eagle can be seen above a portal. This is the emblem of Castruccio Castracani (1281-1328), who after taking and sacking Lucca would subsequently become lord of the city (see below). The present location of the fresco is the result of various alterations to the building, which was originally acquired by Castruccio Casrtracani in 1324. In 1539 the tower which housed a powder magazine blew up after being hit by lightning, causing such extensive damage that the entire palazzo was rebuilt, but various surviving parts of the old structure were retained, including this portal.

The Cortile degli Svizzeri takes it name from the fact that, from 1653 to 1806, it lodged the corps of Swiss soldiers responsible for guarding the palazzo. Recruited in the canton of Lucerne, each of these soldiers had to be a practising Catholic. This decision to hire Swiss soldiers was taken after the treacherous murder of captain Pietro Costantino da Fermo by a member of the previous guard corps, which had comprised fugitive, exiles, and those whose misdeeds were considered to be "crimes of honour."

CASTRUCCIO CASTRACANI

Born in Lucca in 1281 to a Ghibelline family, Castruccio Castracani degli Antelminelli was later driven out of the city by the rival faction of the Neri. He then lived as an exile in England, where his valour brought him to the attention of King Edward II, but he had to leave that country after a "crime of honour." Back in Tuscany, he entered the service of Uguccione della Faggiuola, under whom he would take part in the sack of his native city. After various vicissitudes, Castracani was imprisoned by Uguccione, who feared him as a rival. However, when Faggiuola had to flee as a result of popular uprisings in Pisa and Lucca, the people of his native city set Castracani free and appointed him as Captain of the city, then Consul for Life (1316). He spent the remainder of his life administering his territories and resisting the encroachments of Florence and its allies.

SILK MARKS ❾

Church of San Cristoforo
Via Fillungo - 55100 Lucca

Museo Nazionale di Villa Guinigi. Via della Quarquonia. 55100 Lucca (LU)
• Tel/Fax: 0583 49 60 33
• Opening hours: Tuesday to Saturday 8.30-19.30, Sunday 8.30-13.30. Closed on Monday, Christmas Day, New Year's Day and 1 May.
• Admission: 4 €, reduced: 2 €, free for those under 18 and over 65. Joint ticket with the Museo Nazionale di Palazzo Mansi: 6.50 €, reduced: 3.25 €.

Evidence of the time when Lucca was a centre of silk trade

A particularly sharp-eyed visitor might notice a rust mark on the façade of the church of San Cristoforo. Evidence of the time when Lucca was a centre of the silk trade, this was caused by two perpendicular rods of iron which used to serve as standard by which to measure the tools used in making silk. Dating from 1290 and measuring 45 and 86 centimetres respectively, these measures (used in determining the width of combs and looms) are now stored in the Museum of Villa Guinigi. Other silk trade "standards" can be seen at the church of San Frediano (page 195). From the 11th century onwards, the manufacture and sale of silk was the basis for Lucca's wealth. Given that the pre-eminence of the town depended upon the skill of silk-wavers, their craft was surrounded by mystery and its secrets were under no circumstances to be communicated to outsiders. In order to control and safeguard their craft, weavers and silk-merchants formed a Merchants' Tribunal (Corte dei Mercanti). This met in the church of San Cristoforo at the end of Via Fillungo, which still remains the city's main shopping street.

SILK

Silk is made from the cocoons of the silkworm, which are smothered and then soaked in boiling water in order to kill the chrysalis without damaging the case containing it. The unravelled threads from around a dozen or so cocoons are then spun together to form a single thread of silk. This is strengthened in a subsequent process known as throwing, with the silk being de-gummed (i.e. stripped of remaining mucilage) by being soaked again in boiling soapy water. After that comes the dyeing and weaving. The whole process was developed by the Chinese in the 17th century BC, and the secret would be jealously guarded for almost three thousand years. However travellers (and spies) brought back to Europe information which made it possible to begin copying the technique from around the 6th century AD. With the advent of industrialisation in the 19th century, the manufacture of silk in Europe would almost entirely disappear, in part because of epidemics which killed the silkworms or the mulberry trees on which they fed, in part due to Asian countries taking advantage of these circumstances to reassert a near-monopoly over the silk trade.

MODERN PORTRAITS ON THE FAÇADE OF THE CHURCH OF SAN MICHELE IN FORO ❿

Piazza San Michele - 55100 Lucca (LU)

> **How Cavour and Garibaldi come to find themselves on the façade of a 13th century church...**

The famous church of San Michele in Foro is celebrated by townsfolk and tourists alike; however there are some rather tasty little details about the place which they may not know.

The restoration of the building began in 1866, at the height of enthusiasm for the unification of Italy. Working on the small columns in the upper part of the façade, the craftsmen of the day replaced the badly damaged heads with portraits of contemporary figures – that is, with heroes of the Risorgimento. Thus the sharp-eyed – or those equipped with a good pair of binoculars – can make out Garibaldi (third figure from the right, in the second row from the bottom); Cavour (alongside), King Vittorio Emanuele II (seventh figure from the right), and Mazzini (fourth figure from the left) – not forgetting the great mediaeval poet Dante (sixth from the left).

At little higher up, at the very top of the façade, the large statue of St. Michael holds in its left hand a ring with a red stone which, it is said, reflects the light of the sun into the eyes of anyone who happens to be standing in front of the Banca Commerciale in Piazza San Michele around noon. Legend has it that all those who see this light and make a wish will see it come true…

What is definitely true is that the angel's wings are made up of "mobile" feathers, so that the wind can pass through them and not blow against them as into a sail.

Finally, on the right side of the cathedral, recent restoration work has been careful not to remove the graffiti which over the course of the years was scratched by the market traders who brought their produce here to sell.

WINDOWS FOR CHILDREN

Finistrelle are small windows which enabled children to see outside without any risk of falling. A good number of such *finistrelle* can be seen in Piazza del Salvatore (number 9), Corte Portici and Via Calderia (numbers 19 and 21).

MUSEO PAOLO CREASCI AND THE HISTORY OF ITALIAN EMIGRANTS

⓫

Via Vittorio Emanuele, 3 - 55100 Lucca (LU)
• Tel: 0583 41 74 83
• E-Mail: info@fondazionepaolocresci.it • www.fondazionepaolocresci.it
• Opening hours: from 1 October to 30 April, 9.30-12.30 and 14.30-17.30; 1 May to 30 September, 10.00-12.30 and 15.00-18.30. Closed on Monday
• Free admission.

They Dreamt of "La'Merica"!

Not identified by any sign or plaque on its outside walls, the Museo Paolo Cresci is undoubtedly the least known of the museums in Lucca. It charts the phenomenon of Italian emigration. Comprising the spartan objects used by emigrants – cardboard boxes, robust leather suitcases, bundles, and large bags crammed with souvenirs – the collection gives a very moving picture of how those far from the motherland recreated a sense of home, perhaps within some sort of "Little Italy".* The photographs are a particularly striking record of the brutal reality faced by those who took ship for the long desired 'Merica, where the emigrants first experience would be the harsh immigration controls they had to go through on Ellis Island, beneath the shadow of the Statue of Liberty…

The museum does not provide a nostalgic view of emigration and does not hide the fact that the main motive behind it was poverty. As their only capital was their labour, the immigrants accepted any sort of job, which resulted in them often being looked down upon – be it in the Americas or in France. Trials and tribulations, successes and disappointments, happiness and sadness – the whole mystery of human life is portrayed in this engaging museum.

"AN INDULGENCE OF FORTY DAYS FOR THOSE WHO SAY THREE HAIL MARYS"

Like a number of other cities in Italy – for example, Palermo – Lucca provides devout Catholics with easily-obtained indulgences for their sins. One sees numerous plaques offering indulgences in the streets and both within and on the exterior of churches. Look, for example, at the side of the church of San Leonardo dei Borghi or at Via del Portico. In the latter case, the indulgence is associated with an ex-voto tabernacle of the Virgin and Child. This was raised in thanks for the safe landing of a child who fell from the fourth floor of a building without serious injury. The panel reads "Indulgence of Forty Days for those who say three Hail Marys." An indulgence is the total or partial remission granted by God from the pains of Purgatory, and it is obtained by some act of piety (a pilgrimage, prayer, or act of self-mortification) performed in a spirit of repentance. Even if the whole thing may strike many as amazing, belief in this system of indulgences still thrives within the Catholic Church.

---

* "Little Italy" was the name given in the United States to the neighbourhoods which contained a concentration of lodgings occupied by Italian immigrants. Overcrowded and uncomfortable, these apartment buildings gave new arrivals the opportunity to provide each other with mutual assistance, and to maintain some of the values and customs of home.

PROLVAT VT CVLPAM DAT VIRGO
SANGVINIS VNDAM
AT CADIT IGNORANS IMPIVS
ESSE PIAM

A YAWNING GULF OF HELL IN THE CHURCH OF SAN AGOSTINO ⓬

Piazza San Agostino
55100 Lucca (LU)

> *The Madonna of the Pebble*

The church of San Agostino was built in the 14th century on the site of an old Augustine monastery; its bell-tower incorporates the arches of an ancient Roman theatre. A side chapel in the right aisle has a painting referred to as "The Madonna of the Pebble" because of a miraculous event that astonished the faithful of the time. One day an inhabitant of the city who had just lost a large sum of money gambling was returning home full of bitterness and vented his anger by throwing a pebble at an image of the Virgin. This immediately began to bleed, and a yawning gulf opened up to swallow the unfortunate blasphemer.

The event is commemorated by a plaque in the chapel. Directly below it is an iron trap door over the opening through which the wretched man is said to have fallen straight into Hell…

SIGHTS NEARBY:

THE MADONNA DEL SOCCORSO ⓭

Via Fillungo, 215

Near Piazza San Pietro, at 215 Via Fillungo, is a raised shrine with an alto rilievo of the Madonna del Soccorso [Our Lady of Succour], in which the Virgin wields a stick to defend the Infant Jesus from the Devil.

The veneration of Our Lady of Succour owes its origins to a miracle that occurred in Sciacca (Sicily), where a mother exasperated at the behaviour of her six-year-old child told him to "go to the Devil." Satan, always on the look-out for such occasions, immediately appeared and seized the child. In response to an appeal for help from the distraught mother, the Virgin appeared robed in white and gold; wielding a club, she then crushed the Devil at her feet whilst protecting the child beneath her cloak. Veneration of Our Lady of Succour was further encouraged by the miraculous healing of the monk Nicolò Bruno (again in Sciacca).

A PHIAL OF CHRIST'S BLOOD IN THE CHURCH OF SAN FREDIANO ⓮

Piazza San Frediano
55100 Lucca (LU)

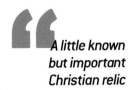

A little known but important Christian relic

If the story of the journey which brought the Holy Visage to Europe is widely told (see page 175), fewer people are aware that the same ship carrying that crucifix from the Holy Land also brought with it phials of Christ's blood.

When the boat ran aground at Luni (Liguria), it was found to contain not only the Holy Visage but also two phials of Christ's blood. One of these was kept for a time at Luni. Later, when the seat of the diocese was moved from that town to Sarzana in 1204, the phial went there too; it is still to be found in the Cathedral dell'Assunta in Sarzana. The second phial is now in Lucca, in the Cenami Chapel in the church of San Frediano (to the right as you enter). A little known but important Christian relic, it is put on display for the faithful only once a year, on Good Friday.

> The iron cross on the façade of the church is a reproduction of the standard measures for the silk industry which could once be seen on the façade of the church of San Cristoforo (see page 187).

SIGHTS NEARBY:

VESTIGES OF A ROMAN AMPHITHEATRE ⓯

17, Piazza dell'Anfiteatro

The elliptical shape of Piazza dell'Anfiteatro is due to the fact that the square was laid out on the remaining terraces of a Roman amphitheatre dating from the 2nd/1st century BC. Some of the decoration of that original structure also survives here: at eye-level on the façade of no. 17 one can see a small part of the original decorative frieze. Walking round the square by Via dell'Anfiteatro one can also see some other remnants of the Roman structure: not only some large stone blocks from the base but also some sections of brick partitioning walls.

MONOLITH IN THE CHURCH OF SAN FREDIANO ⑯

Piazza San Frediano
55100 Lucca (LU)

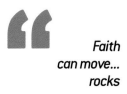

*Faith
can move...
rocks*

To the left of the high altar in the church of San Frediano is an imposingly large rock of white marble (five metres by two), which has been carved into the form of a rectangular block resting on four feet (two of them the hooves of oxen). A Latin plaque above the stone says "You who read this, whoever you are, you are of stone if this stone does not lead you to admire and venerate San Frediano."

The rock comes from the quarry of San Lorenzo at Vaccoli, on the slopes of the hills between Lucca and Pisa, and its exceptional size made it perfect for the bishop, San Frediano [St. Finnian], who was looking for a single piece of stone to serve as the altar. But a problem arose over how the stone was to be transported, as no one could manage to lift it. It was then that San Frediano miraculously intervened: after intense prayer, he lifted the stone as if it were no more than a sheet of paper and placed it on the cart that was to carry it to its destination. Later, when the church was altered, the block of marble was stored in the sacristy and forgotten. Rediscovered in the 16th century, it was then placed where we see it today.

Note that this was not first miracle performed by the Irish-born St. Frediano: it was he who by means of a simple rake diverted the course of the river Serchio which regularly flooded Lucca.

THE FIRST KNOWN DEPICTION OF THE EARTH AS ROUND

Painted in 1506 by Amico Aspertini, the fresco in the chapel of St. Augustine in the church of San Frediano portrays the journey that brought the Holy Visage from Luni to Lucca (see page 175). When one looks closely, one notes that there are numerous vessels present within the pictorial space and that only the upper parts of the ones furthest away are visible. Furthermore, the line of the horizon is clearly marked so as to accentuate this impression.

It is therefore said that this fresco is the first known representation in art of the rotundity of the Earth. The claim is plausible, given that the fresco was painted in 1506 – that is, 14 years after Christopher Columbus's first voyage to America. The Genoese navigator was, in fact, convinced on that occasion that he had touched land in India, having travelled "to the East via the West". By that time the rotundity of the Earth was a recognised fact amongst the educated and the learned, and was becoming increasingly accepted by the populace at large.

THE WATER TOWERS OF THE LUCCA AQUEDUCT ⑰

Via del Tempietto - 55100 Lucca (LU)
Via di San Quirico in Guamo Guamo - 55060 Capannoro (LU)

*Aesthetics
and engineering*

The neo-classical water tower/temple at San Concordio, just a short distance from the Lucca city walls, is a structure of rare elegance. Comprising a rotunda and a colonnade, it forms a spectacular composition when viewed along with the arches of the aqueduct that run towards one corner of the structure. Rather more austere (and without a colonnade), the Guamo water tower is built against the hillside. Both bear evidence to the clear importance of aesthetic considerations in the construction of the Lucca aqueduct. Built under the supervision of the architect Lorenzo Nottolini in the period 1823-1851, the aqueduct carries water into the area from the northern slopes of Monte Pisano. After passing through filtering and purifying processes, the water is then stored in the Guamo water tower. The next section of the aqueduct itself is made up of 400 brick arches that stretch for a total of 3,250 metres; however, its continuous line is today interrupted by the motorway. Once the water reaches the San Concordio water tower, it flows into a large marble reservoir from which it then passes to the city via two large steel channels.

THE LEGEND OF LUCCA'S BOTANICAL GARDEN

Legend has it that, on moonless nights, one can hear the lamentations of the ghost of Lucida Manso echoing across the lake within the Botanical Garden. Rich and beautiful, this young woman is said to have chosen her lovers during the course of sumptuous banquets. After having had her way with them, she would then dispose of them by throwing them down a blade-lined well shaft which was hidden beneath a trap-door. Supposedly so narcissistic she even had a mirror concealed in her breviary to admire herself at prayers, Lucida was horrified one day to discover a wrinkle when she inspected her reflection. In despair, she made a pact with the Devil, who appeared to her in the guise of a young man. In exchange for an extra thirty years of youth, she gave him her soul. When the thirty years were about to end, the woman climbed to the top of the clock tower in Via Fillungo in a desperate attempt to stop the clock hands reaching the fatal hour. But the devil caught up with her and took her on a ride around the city walls in a flaming chariot before disappearing with his prize into the lake of the Botanical Garden. Although this may be a legend, Lucida Mansio certainly existed and lived in Lucca during the 17th century. Only 22 years old when her first husband, Vincenzo Diversi, was murdered, she then re-married, but her second spouse, Gaspare Mansi, died shortly afterwards of the plague. It was said that she was beautiful and capricious and had no qualms about taking lovers. No doubt the tale grew out of jealousy, leading certain people to exaggerate accounts of her behaviour.

A STROLL THROUGH ART NOUVEAU LUCCA ⓮

55100 Lucca (LU)

> **The other architectural jewels of Lucca**

Famous for its Renaissance city walls, Lucca's numerous Art Nouveau villas have received much less attention. In 1870 the City council took ownership of the walls and undertook a programme of urban expansion in the areas beyond. The new lots of land were purchased by the local bourgeoisie, who used these sites mainly for building luxurious villas. In a style that varied between the neo-classical and the Art Nouveau, these new districts are well worth a visit, particularly for the villas mentioned below.

The highest concentration of Art Nouveau-style villas is to be found along the southern section of the ring road: Viale G. Guisti, Viale Cavour and Viale G. Carducci. In the latter avenue, note at number 627 a villa decorated with neo-Florentine motifs inspired by the art of the 15th century; today, this is home to the Symphonic Music School. Slightly further on, at nos. 523-545, is a villa whose elegant curve follows a slight bend in the avenue. At the end of Viale Carducci one should not fail to make the detour to Via Pascoli, where at no. 97 there is a superb corner house called Villa Dinelli (formerly Villa Malerbi). Built by Modesto Orzali and his son Gaetano, Villa Ducloz at no. 234 Via Matteo Civitali is a very original structure designed around a large circular panel surrounded by sunflower motifs; the house would subsequently be known as Villa Dianda and is now Villa Barsanti.

Within the city walls a certain number of shops have also preserved Art Nouveau décors. For the central pharmacy, at the corner of Via Beccheria and Piazza San Michele, the ceramicist Umberto Pinzauti created a number of lascivious and at times ambiguous little angels; though in an Art Nouveau style, they are produced using a technique that recalls the work of the Della Robbia family. Passing down the city's main shopping street, Via Fillungo, one often encounters magnificent shop signs and frontages that still reflect the period of the late 19th and early 20th century. See, for example, the Chicchetti jewellery shop at number 219, and the jeweller's and goldsmith's shop, Pellegrini, at no. 111.

One of the least well-known traces of Art Nouveau in Lucca is to be found in the church of San Leonardo in Borghi (Via San Leonardo), where an entire chapel dedicated to the Virgin is decorated in this style.

NORTH WEST

STANDARD MEASURES FROM THE 16TH CENTURY

❶

L'Arringo
55051 Barga (LU)
The Arringo is a meadow to the right of the cathedral. It takes its name from the town assembly which met there; the etymology of the word being the same as that of "harangue".

ust to the left of Barga cathedral, the loggia in front of the old Palazzo del Podestà (now the municipal museum) houses standards of weights and measures that were used in the 16th century.

Under the loggia, a bushel...

The first of these is the classic Florentine braccia, which measured 58.3 cm. The second is much more unusual and interesting because it reveals a curious fact about this period: people were allowed to walk around carrying daggers and swords, as long as their length respected fixed standards. This measure, known as il coltello (the knife), gives the maximum length of a knife blade at one quarter of a braccia – that is, 14.5 cm.

Two other measures are fixed in the wall and were used to measure dry goods (corn and flour). The largest of these was the staio fiorentino (the Florentine bushel) which measured 24.4 litres, whilst the half staio measured 12.2 litres. See Pisa, page 163, for a history of the passage to the metric system and the correspondences between the old weights and measures and the new system.

SIGHTS NEARBY:

SYMBOLS IN BARGA CATHEDRAL

❷

Barga's cathedral stands near the Palazzo del Podestà. To the right of its main

doorway is a curious stone, no doubt 'recycled' here from its original location. It bears an inscription of certain familiar symbols, but whose significance in this case is rather mysterious. It might, however, be a signature left by the master masons who worked on the cathedral; the same exact inscription is to be found on the Baptistery in Piazza dei Miracoli in Pisa (see page 153).

CRYSTALS ASSOCIATED WITH CARRARA MARBLE ❸

The Fornaci di Barga Mineralogy and Palaeontology Group
Via Galilei Galileo
55051 Fornaci di Barga (LU)
• Tel: 0583 758 879 • Visits by appointment only.
• Free admission.

Diamond in marble

While the main attraction of other marbles is their variety of colour, Carrara marble has the unique characteristic of being of a very pure white. This means that the stone brings out all the magnificence of any other minerals found within it – particularly if these are crystallised. These juxtapositions form striking visual contrasts and are much sought after by collectors and enthusiasts of natural curios.

Founded in 1973, the Fornaci di Barga Mineralogy and Palaeontology Group specialises in the search for such mineral combinations within local marble. On its premises there is an exceptional collection of some 50 different types, along with fossils and minerals from all over the world.

One exhibit is a superb piece of rock crystal occurring within a milky white chunk of marble; the stunning contrast of the two materials reminds one of the mysterious chances at work in natural creation. Another exhibit is a crystal of pure sulphur (unmixed with other elements); bright yellow in colour, this stands out against the marble like a flower under ice.

The honorary president of the Group, Raffaleo Lucchesi, is happy to open the museum to visitors (by prior appointment). Far from being too busy to assist, he welcomes the chance to give you a knowledgeable tour, and – photos in hand – will gladly tell you where he and his friends found these natural wonders.

THE LEGEND OF THE DEVIL'S BRIDGE

Ponte del Diavolo or Ponte della Maddalena. 55023 Borgo a Mozzano (LU)
The spectacular humpback bridge over the river Serchio has five arches in all; the one at the end was added more recently to span the local rail line. The nickname Ponte del Diavolo comes from a legend dating from the time of its construction in the 14th century. Work had fallen behind schedule and so the architect – fearing he would not meet the deadline – called for help from the Devil. Lucifer agreed to complete the structure overnight as long as it was agreed he could carry off the soul of the first person to cross the bridge. Stricken with remorse, the architect confessed what he had done to the village priest, who hit upon a solution: a pig would be the first living creature to cross the bridge... Furious, the Devil disappeared into the river beneath in a cloud of sulphur. It is also said that the Devil later got his revenge by making sure that there were constant increases in the toll required to cross the bridge.

THE BRANCOLINO ON THE CHURCH
OF SAN GIORGIO

❹

Pieve di Brancoli
55100 Lucca (LU)

*Who is
that odd
character on
the Church of
San Giorgio?*

According to some sources, the church of San Giorgio in Pieve di Brancoli was first founded in 722; what is certain is that there was a church here in 1097. Above the side door to the right of the church there is a carved figure that does not fit in with the usual iconography of religious sculpture. Nicknamed Il Brancolino (from the verb meaning "to grope one's way"), this unusual bas-relief is still a mystery. The most likely explanation offered nowadays is that it was carved as a joke by one of the stone-masons who built the church.

SIGHTS NEARBY:

THE VILLAGE OF PARIS (BORGO PARIGI)

❺

Villa di Camigliano or Villa Torrigiani

3, Via del Gomberaio

55010 Camigliano Santa Gemma (LU)

Borgo Parigi is located outside the villa grounds and so is open to visitors.

Opening hours for the club: Tuesday to Friday 20.00-dusk,

Saturday 13.30-midnight, Sunday 9.00-midnight. Closed Monday.

Villa Torrigiani, open every day from 1 March to second Sunday in November, 10.00-13.00 and 15.00-sunset.

For confirmation of opening hours: phone 0583 92 80 41 or e-mail villatorrigiani@villelucchesi.net

At Camigliano, the birthplace of St. Gemma Galgani, stands Villa Torrigiani, one of the numerous villas dotted around the countryside outside Lucca. In the 17th century Nicolao Santini, ambassador of the Republic of Lucca at the court of Louis XIV, had the villa transformed. The gardens were laid out according designs and drawings by Le Nôtre, hence the place's nickname of "Little Versailles." It is therefore hardly surprising that the hamlet housing the villa staff and estate workers (located outside the main gateway) should be named Parigi (Paris). Nowadays the Parigi Circolo Sportivo [Sports Club] attracts local members and the occasional tourist...

Another justification for the name Parigi is that the towers in the hamlet functioned as pigeon lofts for the "Parisian" carrier pigeons which Nicolao Santini used for communication with his French embassy. These pigeons could only fly in a single direction – back to the loft where they were raised.

PINOCCHIO'S OAK TREE
"IL QUERCIONE" (LITERALLY "GREAT OAK")

Via Carrara. The Wood of San Martino in Colle
55012 Capannori (LU)

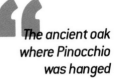

The ancient oak where Pinocchio was hanged

Take the Altopascio exit off the A11 motorway (Firenze-Mare) which links Florence with the coast, then drive towards the village of Montecarlo. Once there, take Via di San Martino, which leads up to the church of San Martino in Colle. From the church take the road on the left (the road surfacing ends after a few metres). The oak tree is to be found after a couple of left turns. Even though there is no notice or sign you will recognise it immediately because of its spectacular and majestic size.

Known as either Pinocchio's Oak or *Il Quercione* ('The Great Oak'), this remarkable tree is more than 600 years old. It is said to have inspired the scene in which Collodi's famous hero is hanged by the Cat and the Fox.

Unfortunately, the oak is being attacked by parasites which threaten its very life. But a campaign to save it has recently been launched by the local council of Capannori. One of the supporters of that campaign is Roberto Benigni, director of one of the most recent film adaptations of Collodi's famous children's story.

PINOCCHIO AND CARLO COLLODI

Carlo Lorenzini is better known as Carlo Collodi (the nom de plume is taken from the name of his mother's birthplace, a village where he himself spent childhood holidays). Collodi was born in Florence in 1826 and after having fought for Italian independence, he worked primarily in the field of publishing. He created the character of Pinocchio in 1881 for a children's comic. After the innumerable protests which the publishers received following Pinocchio's death by hanging in Chapter 15, Collodi would resurrect his famous character in *The Adventures of Pinocchio: The Story of a Puppet*, which is still a bestseller and generates a whole range of merchandising throughout Italy. In the village of Collodi there is now a famous Pinocchio Park.

SIGHTS NEARBY:

THE PLAQUE AND THE MAGNOLIA OF THE SWISS GUARDS

Piazza Vittorio Emanuele - 55011 Altopascio (LU)

In September 1505, 150 Swiss halberdiers left Bellinzone in the Swiss canton of Tessin for Rome, called there by Pope Julius II. They would arrive in the city on 22 January 1506, becoming the first body of the Papal Swiss Guard.

In 2006, to commemorate the five-hundredth anniversary of the creation of that Papal Guard, the 720-kilometres march was repeated by 70 former Swiss Guards. At each stopping-point on their route, a plaque was placed by a tree. Under the magnolia in Piazza Vittorio Emanuele, the plaque records that on 20 April 2006 the march reached its 14th stopping-place at Altopascio, having already covered some 293 kms.

A PERFECT COPY OF
THE *MADONNA DEL BALDACCHINO*

8

Cathedral of Pescia
Piazza Duomo

*A certain air
of déjà vu*

Turning into the last chapel on the right (the Turini Chapel), visitors might begin to wonder: "I'm sure I've seen that painting someplace else!" And you may have very well seen it before: in the Pitti Palace in Florence. The story behind this magnificent copy of Raphael's Madonna del Baldacchino is rather amusing. At the beginning of the 16th century, Cardinal Baldassare Turini, a native of Pescia, commissioned Raphael to paint a picture for the church of Santa Maria Assunta in his native town. In 1507 the painting was given a triumphant reception by the faithful and thereafter became the pride of the church.

However, in 1697, Prince Fernando de Medici, the eldest son of Grand Duke Cosimo III and a great lover of art, visited Pescia and was left thunderstruck by Raphael's masterpiece. To persuade the local clergy to let him have it, he offered not only the immense sum of 1,000 scudi but also commissioned the talented artist Pietro Dandini to paint a copy that was as close as possible to the original. The two paintings were then switched - in great secrecy - during the night of 7 September 1697.

The local clergy later used the money they had received to install a church organ and to extend their library.

SIGHTS NEARBY:

MERIDIAN IN THE CATHEDRAL OF PESCIA **9**

Piazza del Duomo

The improvements carried out thanks to the money received from Prince Ferdinand (see above) also affected the large sundial meridian that runs across the floor of the church. Whilst part of the white marble line is still visible, one now has to open the door in the enclosure beneath the organ to see it in its entirety. The hole by which sunlight entered the church and fell onto the meridian had already been moved during the course of previous building work, so that the sundial was even then no longer as precise as it had once been.

A DA VINCI ANGEL

⑩

Church of San Gennaro
Via Ilio Menicucci
55010 San Gennaro (LU)
To visit, ask at the presbytery, to the left of the church

One of Leonardo da Vinci's two known works of sculpture

Standing on the steep main road that runs through the hills above Lucca, the village of San Gennaro is not far from Collodi (which provided the writer Carlo Lorenzini, author of The Adventures of Pinocchio, with his penname). Re-built in the 12th century, the church of San Gennaro would in 1998 become an unusual focus of attention for the world's media. In an article published in the Italian newspaper Il Sole 24 ore, Professor Carlo Pedretti of UCLA, the greatest living expert on Leonardo da Vinci, would attribute the statue of a angel in San Gennaro to that artist.

The revelation was something of a scoop, as at the time there was only one known work of sculpture by Leonardo da Vinci: that of the Christ Child, now kept in the vaults of a bank in Rome.

This polychrome terracotta statue of an angel had in 1958 been attributed to the "School of Verrocchio" by Prof. Lodovico Ragghianti, an art historian and critic. Given that the young Leonardo learnt his craft in Verrocchio's studio, Ragghianti was not far off the presently accepted attribution. The basis for identifying this statue as an early work by Leonardo is its striking similarity with his sketch "Study for the Sleeve of the Angel of the Annunciation" which is now in the Uffizi in Florence.

What remains a mystery is how this work by Leonardo da Vinci ended up in this modest village. However that came about, there are records of its presence here from 1772 onwards: archives record that the statue was damaged that year by a falling ladder. Having been restored on that occasion by a local artist, the statue still retains all its charm.

THE EMBLEM OF THE ORDER OF THE CROSS OF SAINT ANTHONY

Piazza Ospitalieri
55011 Altopascio (LU)
• A sign on the A11 motorway (Firenze-Mare) which informs drivers that they are approaching the town of Altopascio mentions "bread and board" (pane e ospitalità). This was, in fact, a traditional service offered by Altopascio, a necessary stopping-point on the ancient Via Francigena (see page 74). One can still see various important reminders of this past function in the town's historic centre.

The order of the Tau

I n various places there are traces of the emblem associated with the Knights of the Order of St. Anthony: the Greek "T" or Tau (see box feature below). The first of these (a large stone from the knights' old hospital) is on the balcony of the Municipal Library overlooking Piazza Ospitalieri; the building is entered by a staircase that runs down into the large Piazza Vittorio Enmanuele. There are also several other Greek Ts , together with ancient carved inscriptions, to be found on the stone facing of the north side of the church bell tower.

KNIGHTS OF THE ORDER OF THE CROSS OF SAINT ANTHONY

The Altopascio Hospital was founded in the 11th century; some argue the tenth. It was intended to offer board, food and care for the numerous pilgrims taking this road on their way to the tomb of St. Peter in Rome (then perhaps continuing to the Holy Land) or, travelling in the other direction, on their way to Santiago di Compostella. So that these travellers would not lose their way in the unhealthy marshlands of this area, at nightfall the local bell tower (still in use today) rang La Smarrita, which take its name from the verb "to go astray." Due to the fact that travellers were preyed upon by brigands and bandits, the Augustinian monks who ran the hospital soon had to arm themselves in order to provide protection. This was the origin of the oldest military order in the world: the Hospitaller Knights of the Cross of Saint Anthony, also known as the Order of the Tau because of the Greek "T" that was their symbol. The symbol was traced in white on the left side of the black or grey robes worn by the Knights. The Tau was a symbol of both the pilgrim's staff and the Cross of Christ.

Altopascio still maintains its reputation for hospitality; the town has eight free places to provide board for visitors to its monasteries. Contact the Tourist Office (10, Piazza Garibaldi - 55011 Altopascio (LU); tel/fax: 0583 21 65 25; e-mail: turismo@comune.altopascio.lu.it) or the local library (23, Piazza Vittorio Emanuele; tel/fax: 0583 21 62 80; e-mail : biblioteca@ comune.altopascio.lu.it).

CROSS OF THE PASSION IN THE CHURCH OF SAN PIETRO IN GRADO ⓬

Basilica of San Pietro al Molo
5, Via Vecchia di Marina - 56010 San Piero a Grado (PI)
• Tel: 050 960065
• Opening hours: 8.00-19.00
• Free admission.

> *A Cross with the instruments of Christ's Passion*

Supposedly built on the exact site where St. Peter the Apostle came ashore after his voyage from Palestine, the church of San Pietro in Grado is curious for a number of reasons. Firstly because it has no actual façade; for unknown reasons, at the end of the 12th/beginning of the 13th century its nave was shortened by a quarter, with the demolished facade being replaced by an enclosed apse. Another curiosity is that the site of the church, now located five kilometres inland, was once a quayside in Pisa, a busy maritime port since Roman times - that is, until gradual silting along the Arno shifted the mouth of the river further west, thus putting an end to the port's usefulness. Inside the church, opposite and a little to the right of the main door, is a very interesting Cross said to date from the 18th century. It is complete with a rare – and surprisingly realistic – depiction of the instruments of the Passion: the hammer, the sponge soaked in vinegar, the Vernicle (a handkerchief impressed with the image of Christ's face), the spear, the ladder, the crown of thorns, the pitcher and bowl used by Pilate when washing his hands, the whip, the red tunic, the chalice, the dice cast by the Roman soldiers and the panel bearing the inscription "INRI" [Jesus of Nazareth, King of the Jews]. The only things missing are the nails. Another Cross with a powerful evocation of the Passion is to be seen at Montecatini Alto (see page 76).

THE PORT OF PISA WIPED OFF THE MAP

Porto Pisano, the ancient port of Pisa, dated back at least as far as the 6th century BC; archaeological evidence shows that by this period the city was trading with the Greeks, the Phoenicians, and the Gauls. The docks of the port ran from just north of modern-day Livorno to the vast estuary of the Arno and the Auser (a river that has since run dry) in an area that has now silted up. Jealously protected by the maritime republic, the port played a major role in the development of Pisa; it was defended by four immense towers that were destroyed by the Genoese during the battle of La Meloria in 1290 but then rebuilt in 1297-1310. However, pressure from foreign naval powers and conflicts with neighbouring cities and rivals initiated a long period of decline for Pisa. The port did continue to function, but less and less attention was devoed to the upkeep of the docks. Finally, the Florentine conquest of Pisa in 1509 and the decision to build the new port of Leghorn [Livorno] delivered the coup de grâce. Without regular maintenance, the port gradually silted up thanks to the alluvial deposits left by the Arno. Now, less than five centuries later, the sea is some 5 km from the original coastline.

MONUMENT TO THE VIAREGGIO DEEP-SEA DIVERS⓯

Lungo Canale Palombari dell'Artiglio
55049 Viareggio (LU)

*Pioneers
in the recovery
of sunken cargo*

With advances in the technique and technology of deep-sea diving, people began to contemplate the possibility of recovering cargoes lost in shipwreck at sea. In 1925 a company was founded in Genoa to carry out such deep-water salvage, and nearly all the divers it employed would come from Viareggio.

The first attempted salvage – involving the diving ship *Artiglio* – was only half-successful, but it attracted a lot of attention because the divers shattered the existing record for deep-water submersion, reaching a depth of 136 m. Their intention had been to recover the twelve tons of ivory tusks and 13,000 carats of diamonds which had been on board the *Elisabethville*, a ship torpedoed by a German U-Boat in 1917. Only the ivory was brought up to the surface; of the diamonds, no trace.

In 1930 the company suffered the tragic loss of the Artiglio, along with its crew and all divers, during a mission to destroy the cargo of munitions that had been on board the American ship *Florence*.

The Viareggio divers' greatest triumph, however, would come shortly afterwards, when they recovered part of the gold that had been in the hold of the English ship *Egypt*, that sank off the coast of Brittany. A packet boat that travelled from London to Bombay, the ship had collided in thick fog with the French cargo vessel *La Seine* in 1922. Thanks to the diving-bell designed by head diver Alberto Gianni and engineer Roberto Galeazzi, the divers on Artiglio II managed to bring to the surface a total of 856 ingots. Amongst the other operations in which they were involved, one that deserves anecdotal mention is the refloating of Giacomo Puccini's yacht, the *Ciò Ciò San*.

THE DIVING-BELL

The monument in Viareggio includes one of the diving-bells used in the deep-sea recoveries. The bell was lowered by cable directly above the wreck. Inside, the diver communicated with the surface via phone, guiding a scoop operated by a crane. In the case of the Egypt, the ship's strongroom had to be blown open using explosives, again following instructions provided by the diver in the bell.

ARCICONFRATERNITÀ DELLA MISERICORDIA ⑭

97, Via Cavalotti. 55049 Viareggio (LU)
• Don'tt forget to take one of the free leaflets on "Art Nouveau in Tuscany:
Itineraries of Architecture dating from 1880 to 1930", available in the Viareggio
Tourist Office.
• Tourist Office. APT Versilia
• 10, Viale Carducci - 55049 Viareggio (LU)
• Tel : 0584 96 22 33. • E-Mail : aptversilia@versilia.turismo.toscana.it
• www.versilia.turismo.toscana.it

The façade of the Misericordia di Viareggio

The volunteers of the Arciconfratenità de la Misericordia di Viareggio seem rather surprised to see people taking photographs of their premises, which stand some way back from the seafront in a quiet little street; clearly they are used to the beauty of this building's façade. Created by the ceramicists of Galileo Chini's "Fornaci de San Lorenzo," the frontage is quite simply remarkable. On the left, a woman turns towards the past and towards the Cross (which serves as a sort of framework for the entire design), while to the right a woman looks towards the present and seems to be protecting a child. The entire work is in the flamboyant style of Galileo Chini at his most creative.

Viareggio is undoubtedly the Tuscan town with the richest concentration of Art Nouveau architecture; forty or so buildings are listed in the leaflet provided by the Tourist Office. But the terrible fire of 1917 destroyed almost all the wooden buildings along the seashore, with the sole exception of the Padiglione Martini. Having acquired jurisdiction over the seafront, in 1924 the town council decided to redevelop it in a very opulent fashion. A member of the committee of architects responsible for coordinating the scheme, Chini (see below) would leave his own very distinctive mark on the entire project.

GALILEO CHINI

Born in Florence in 1873, Galileo Chini – painter, graphic artist, architect, interior decorator, ceramicist, and set-designer – is considered the most important exponent of Art Nouveau in Italy. After having set up his Arte della Ceramica company for the production of art ceramics in 1896, he would branch out in 1904 by founding I Fornaci di San Lorenzo [Ceramic Kilns of San Lorenzo]. Comprisingceramics, mosaics, glass and also furnishings that incorporated them, Galileo Chini's work would enjoy extraordinary success and win various design awards. In the 1930s Chini would dedicate himself to painting, after having decorated the Throne Room in the Palace of Bangkok; he would also design sets for Puccini's Turandot. He died in Florence in 1956.

The Art Nouveau-style holiday home that he had built for himself at Lido di Camaiore has been preserved and is now a charming little hotel and restaurant: Hotel Villa i Pini, 43, Via Roma - 55043 Lido di Camaiore (LU). Tel: 0584 66 103. E-mail: info@clubipini.com. Site internet : www.clubipini.com. Rooms from 50 € to 170 €. Dinner: 25 € per person (served in the garden upon request).

AN ASCENT ALONG THE PIASTRETA MONORAIL ⑮

Renara, outside Gronda. 54100 Massa-Carrara (MS)
• The "engine" is on display outside the office of the Ezio Ronchieri Marble Works.
It is advisable to phone or send an e-mail beforehand. However, the workcrew are
very happy to show off the wonderful engine for visitors!
16, Via Boschetto. 54100 Massa-Carrara (MS)
• Tel: 0585 41 262 • E-mail: info@ezioronchieri.com

The incredible marble cable car

I n quarrying the famous marble of Massa Carrara, the problem faced by the Ronchieri company was how to get large blocks of immaculate white marble down from an altitude of 1,800 metres. They came up with a spectacular solution: for fifty years – from 1922 to 1972 – the engine now displayed at the entrance to the Ronchieri Marble Works transported blocks of marble weighing up to 12 tons along a monorail that at some points attains a gradient of 80%. The engine was driven by a 22-horsepower motor with five speeds, a reverse gear and pneumatic caterpillar tracks.

The route of the monorail can now be followed on foot. It provides wonderful views, but is not recommended for young children.

Directions: From Massa-Carrara drive towards Gronda. Just before the village, turn right to Renara. Drive for 500 metres until the road comes to an end. Here you are at the point where two mountain streams meet; they are dry in summer. Cross the stream that flows down on your right and then go up the slope on your left, turning to the right of the ruined houses. This brings you to the lower end of the monorail, even if at this level the rail itself has now disappeared. The track looks like a railway line whose two rails have been cemented. Things begin to get more serious once you reach an altitude of 500 metres, with the monorail ascending to 1,800 metres after a steep climb of over three kilometres. Progress over this last part is by means of the steps (2,000 of them!) that run alongside the rail.

A RAMBLE ALONG VIA VANDELLI

Via Vandelli, a historic road linking Modena with the sea, was laid out at the behest of Francesco III d'Este, Duke of Modena (1698- 1780), with the purpose of linking his capital with Massa-Carrara and the sea. The main problem was that the road had to keep within his Duchy and not stray into the neighbouring territories of the Papal States, the Duchy of Lucca or the Grand Duchy of Tuscany. The monk Domenici Vandelli, a geographer and mathematician, was commissioned to chart the road, which was to cross the Apennines at the Tambura Pass (some 1,634 m above sea level). After 13 years of intense work (1738-1751), the road was completed; but it was never used much because of exposed weather conditions and the fact that the surrounding countryside was infested with bandits and brigands. Today, the road is being restored and the route from Resceto to the Tambura Pass is popular with ramblers. A monument placed at the beginning of Via Vandelli commemorates the epic of its creation.

HOMAGE TO SACCO AND VANZETTI   **16**

Piazza Sacco e Vanzetti - 54033 Carrara (MS)
Piazza Sacco e Vanzetti is in front of the Carrara Hospital

Sentenced to death for being anarchists ... and Italian

Gn the side of the square facing the hospital is a small monument inaugurated on 23 August 2006 in memory of Nicola Sacco and Bartolommeo Vanzetti. Above their names are the two words *Gli Anarchici*, with the famous circled "A" that is the symbol of the anarchist movement. The ideas of the anarchists enjoy great support amongst the marble-workers, and the Sacco and Vanzetti affair caused a great stir in the region. The anarchist leader Antonio Meschi is also honoured here by a monument, in Piazza Gramsci.

SACCO AND VANZETTI

Nicola Sacco was born on 22 April 1892 at Torremaggiore in Puglia, and Bartolommeo Vanzetti in Vallifalletto (Piedmont) on 11 June 1888. After emigrating to the United States, they became separately involved with an Italo-American anarchist group, and both took refuge in Mexico to escape the draft (it was there they actually first met). Returning to Massachusetts, they would be accused of a hold-up during which two security guards were killed. After seven years of trials and appeals, they were executed in the electric chair on 23 August 1927, despite protests and the fact that a certain Madeiros had confessed to the crime. In reaction to the executions, veritable riots broke out in London, Paris, and various cities in Germany and Italy; even Benito Mussolini spoke up in the two men's defence. On 23 August 1977, exactly fifty years later, the governor of Massachusetts, Michael Dukakis, would clear their names. The Sacco and Vanzetti affair has inspired a large number of books and films, including Giuliano Montaldo's *Sacco et Vanzetti*. The most famous of the songs inspired by their story is Joan Baez's *Here's to you, Nicola and Bart...*

SIGHTS NEARBY:

ANARCHIST LOGO ON A PLAQUE IN COLONNATA   **17**

Piazza Palestro, Colonnata

In the main town square of Colonnata is a surprising wall plaque commemorating "our Anarchist companions killed on the road to Liberty." Its presence surprises neither local residents nor the region's marble-workers, because anarchism was inseparably bound up with the social struggles fought here from the end of the 19th century onwards. The advent of Fascism would force the anarchists into hiding. When Nazi troops took over the region in 1943, the armed response to their presence would result in fierce reprisals, with the result that after the war the entire province was awarded the Gold Medal for Military Valour.

A PRESERVARLA D... TOTALE ROVINA
QUESTA ROMANA EDICOLA .FU STACCATA
DALLA VETTA DEL FANTI SCRITTI
CUI DIEDE IL NOME
E QUI POSTA NEL GIUGNO 1855

SIGHTS NEARBY:

THE FANTISCRITTI STELE AT THE ART SCHOOL ⓲

Accademia delle Belle Arti. 1, Via Roma. 54033 Carrara (MS)
• Tel: 0585/71658 • Fax: 0585/70295 • E-mail: Info@accademiacarrara.it
• www.accademia.carrara.it
• Visits by appointment only, via contact with the administration at the following
e-mail address: direttore@accademiacarrara.it • Free admission.

Hewn of white marble from one of the most renowned quarries in Carrara –
the the Fantiscritti, to which it gives its name – this Roman stele dates from
the 3rd century AD. It is carved with the figures of Jupiter, Hercules and
Bacchus. These three figures are depicted as nearly naked infants, hence
fantiscritti, which literally means "inscribed with infants" (fanti being a local
word for children). For almost fifteen centuries the stele would remain in the
quarry, serving as a sort of visitors' book for the artists who went there.
Some of the most famous sculptors of their day thus carved their name into
the white marble, including Canova, Giambologna, and Michelangelo. In June
1864 the stele was moved to Palazzo Malaspina for safekeeping; that building now houses the Accademia delle Belle Arti.

MICHELANGELO'S COLUMN IN THE NOSTRA SIGNORA DEL SACRO CUORE OASIS ⓳

502, Via Marconi. 55047 Seravezza (LU) • Tel/Fax: 0584 75 60 36

In 1519 Michelangelo was commissioned by Pope Leo X to design the façade of the
church of San Lorenzo in Florence. In order to save money, the pontiff gave the con-
tract for materials to the quarries of Seravazza instead of to those of Carrara. Thus
Michelangelo went up to Mont Altissimo to supervise the work, getting directly
involved in choosing each piece of marble and then setting to work on the columns
(in spite of the fact that conditions were much more difficult than at Carrara
because the quarry was further away from the coast). Once the columns were finished they were sent to Pisa, from where they were to be shipped up the river Arno
to Florence. In a document dated 2 April 1519 (now in the Notarial Archives in
Carrara), Michelangelo writes: "This Saturday I prepared the hooping of a large column, fifty braccia in length, before it was taken down to the coast. However, a link
in the lewis broke and the column shattered into a hundred pieces in the river
Serra.[...] We all risked getting killed, and we wasted a fine piece of marble..."

One part of that column was subsequently recovered and now stands in the Oasis
Park. The plaque gives the date of its loss as early May – the only way in which it
contradicts the account given in Michelangelo's letter.

But the story did not end there. Due to the delays resulting from having chosen the
quarry at Seravezza, and the rising costs of the project, the façade of San Lorenzo
was abandoned; it would, in fact, never be completed. Michelangelo had other
equally important projects to work on, primarily the tomb of Julius II in Rome. Five
of the twelve columns ordered are said to have been completed. Four of them were
later rediscovered at the Teseco Foundation in Pisa. Only one of the columns ever
reached Florence. Having been laid out in front of the church of San Lorenzo, it
would wait in vain to be raised into place. The story goes that it was subsequently
buried along the right side of the church, where some claim it still lies.

On 18 February 2007 laser lights were used to project onto the front of San Lorenzo
a virtual image of the façade as it appears in Michelangelo's designs.

PIZZERIA-FOCACCERIA IL SELVATICO

㉑

3, Via Fravizzola
Caniparola
54035 Fosdinovo (MS)
• Tel: 0187 67 31 78 or 339 24 49 855
• www.ilselvatico.com

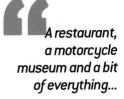

A restaurant, a motorcycle museum and a bit of everything...

Even from the outside it is clear that Il Selvatico is not your usual restaurant: the entire surrounding area is filled with a multitude of objects: bells, vespas, motorcycles, and all kinds of two-wheeled vehicles. Inside, clients have free access to the museum put together by Diego Noce. Here, rooms are given over to the history of motorcycles, musical instruments, and radios, the owner having a passionate interest in anything to do with two-wheeled transport and the world of sound associated with it.

As for food, the pizzeria-focacceria has a range of 35 different types of pizza and 20 types of foccaccia, from 5 €. Cover charge: 1 €. House wine, from 6,50 €.

SIGHTS NEARBY:

㉒

THE BAS-RELIEF OF THE OFFIANO PILGRIM

Offiano Parish Church
54014 Casola in Lunigiana (MS)

Directions: from Aulla take Road S63 towards Reggio Emilia. After 12 kms, turn right onto the S445. After Casola in Lunigiana, the sign to Offiano is a little further on, on the left.

Fitted into the left wall of the church at Offiano is a curious rectangle of white marble. Undoubtedly part of a bas-relief, it shows a pilgrim's scrip, feet and the lower part of his staff. Nowadays, of course, the place is well off the beaten track (to say the least), but this was even the case when pilgrims were travelling along the nearby Via Francigena, the old pilgrimage route which led from

Canterbury, the mother church of English Christendom, to Rome and the tomb of St. Peter (see page 74). Despite this relative isolation, the church at Offiano – which is dedicated to St. Peter and appears in records dating back to 1148 – seems to have been a secondary object of interest to pilgrims, with the adjoining structure apparently being intended to provide accommodation for them.

FOX

1991   2003

RIMARRAI PER SEMPRE
NEI NOSTRI CUORI
RIPOSA IN PACE.
CIAO PICCOLO

PARCO DEGLI AFFETTI

Brunella Nature Park
54011 Aulla (MS)
• Park opening hours: in summer 8.30-19.30, 17.30 in winter. Closed on Monday.

*Italy's first
pet cemetery*

While there were already private burial areas for pets in Lombardy and Emilia Romagna*, the Aulla Parco degli Affetti is the first municipally-owned pet century in Italy; it is, however, run by a private company, not the town council. One must admit that this is a beautiful final resting-place for one's beloved pets, a very calm and serene spot commanding a fine westward view of the valley. Three thousand square metres have been given over to the cemetery and there are already around fifty tombs here, all in either wood or stone (the only materials allowed, for environmental reasons). For around fifty euros (local taxes included), you can acquire a plot, which is yours in perpetuity upon the payment of an annual maintenance charge. Suitable coffins can also be bought. The company running the cemetery can also collect a pet from anywhere in Italy and organise a cremation if that is preferred**.

For a pet burial, apply to :
Parco degli affetti. 22, Via Apua
54011 Aulla (MS)
Tel: 348 44 02 695 (Rita) or 0187 42 19 55
Fax: 0521 89 61 27

Directions: To reach the pet cemetery, enter the park laid out around the castle of La Brunella overlooking the town of Aulla, then go to the last car park near the top. The cemetery is laid out on the slope to the left of the footpath that leads up to the castle. Its entrance is marked by a totem depicting a cat and a dog.

---

* "Il Ponte dell'Arcobaleno" private pet cemetery at Villanova del Sillaro (LO), in Lombardy. Tel: 328 76 94 905 and 320 72 46 070, www.pontedellarcobaleno.it/, e-mail :info@pontedellarcobaleno.it
"Il paradiso di Tom & Jerry" private cemetery for large dogs (but also for hamsters and goldfish) at Altedo (BO), 29, Via Chiavicone. Tel: 0333 38 34 204, fax: 051 87 05 18 www.ilparadisoditomejerry.com

** Dogs, cats and hamsters are accepted, but also 'two-legged' pets: canaries, parrots and other domestic birds.

THE STELES OF LUNIGIANA

Castello di Piagnaro
54027 Pontremoli (MS)
• Tel: 0187 83 14 00
• Opening hours: 1 October to 31 March, 9.00-13.00 and 14.00-17.00;
1April to 30 September, 9.00-13.00 and 14.30-18.30.
•Admission: 3.50 €.

A vast amount of ink has been spilt – and continues to run – about the steles of Lunigiana. Despite the current state of knowledge regarding their origin, their date, and their original location, a number of outrageous or fanciful theories have been put forward regarding them.

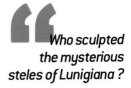

Who sculpted the mysterious steles of Lunigiana ?

Discovered near Pontremoli, these anthropomorphic steles were carved at different periods; the oldest around 2000 BC, the most recent 2,500 years ago. Archaeologists have classified them in three different groups on the basis of how the head is depicted. In the first category, the upper part of the body is simply indicated by the rounded top of the stele; in the second and third categories, the head is distinct from the body, taking the form of a half-moon in those of one group and of a full circle in those of the other.

The statues also indicate gender: the female sculptures have stylised breasts indicated by two small raised disks, whilst the male figures carry a weapon, which is usually held in front of their groin.

The most outrageous theory is based on simple objective observation of the steles, which oddly resemble extra-terrestrials as they appear in works of science fiction…

Naturally enough, historians have favoured that explanation. They argue that these sculptures are consistent with the megalithic sculpture being produced in Europe around this time (the most famous examples of which are menhirs). The female statues are said to depict a mother goddess, whilst the male statues depict the leaders of different clans.

SIGHTS NEARBY:

THE PONTREMOLI LABYRINTHI

Church of San Pietro. Via di Porta Fiorentina. 54027 Pontremoli (MS)

This brick-built church stands on the site of the Benedictine Priory of San Pietro di Conflentu, which was destroyed by Allied bombing in 1944. Upon one of its walls is fixed a stone with a depiction of a labyrinth surmounted by the figures of two knights.

While the labyrinth may be of the same type as that to be seen in the Lucca cathedral (see page 176), here it seems to symbolise the trials and vicissitudes that must be faced by pilgrims. Pontremoli was in fact a stopping-point on the Via Francigena, the main pilgrimage route from Canterbury to Rome (with regard to the Via Francigena, see page 75).

* The name "Lunigiana" comes from that of the town of Luni

FACION OR *FACCION* ON VILLAGE WALLS IN THE LUNIGIANA AREA ㉕

Cervara
54027 Pontremoli (MS)

Faces of mysterious origin

Around Pontremoli, a number of villages in the Lunigiana area contain houses whose walls are adorned with carved faces. Three of these are to be seen in the village of Cervara (in the village high street running parallel to the main road).

Their origin is unknown, but there are those who say that they were carved to protect the inhabitants of the houses from the "Evil Eye."

SIGHTS NEARBY:

MONTEREGGIO, BOOK TOWN ㉖

54026 Mulazzo (MS)

About twenty kilometres from Pontremoli is the small village of Montereggio di Mulazzo, a place which over the years has dedicated itself entirely to the book trade. Every resident here is a bookseller, with an open display of wares outside each house (trust reigns supreme). Though this tradition goes back some way, no one has yet explained how this village became a European distribution point for rare books and those which were banned elsewhere as subversive. In time, people from this village would open bookshops not only in Italy, but also in Spain and in Holland. Others would turn to publishing, founding some of Italy's best-known editorial houses. Furthermore, one of the country's most prestigious literary prizes – the Premio Bancarella [literally, "Bookstall Prize"] – is awarded at Pontremoli, another nearby "Book Town."

LIVORNO
AND SURROUNDINGS

THE TONIETTI FAMILY MAUSOLEUM ❶

GTE
57030 Cavo (LI)

• Directions: from the centre of Cavo go past the castle standing by the beach and follow the one-way system that brings you back to the village by an inland route. Leave the car at the car park just before the back of the castle and then take the GTE (Grande Traversata d'Elba), a wide footpath that starts on the right of the car park and goes towards Monte Grosso. Allow a good twenty minutes to get to the mausoleum up a moderate incline.

The Tomb of the Mining Concession Holders

This Art Nouveau mausoleum was designed by the architect Adolfo Coppedè (1871-1951), whose brother Gino (1866-1927) would lend his name to an entire district of Rome (around Via Dora). Looking like a lighthouse seen from the sea, the monument is built of both local and Carrara marble. Above the entrance is the inscription "Famiglia Tonietti" under a seagull with outstretched wings (some say the bird depicted is an eagle). Very neglected, the mausoleum is in a poor state, and the interior, which contains four tomb openings, is covered in graffiti.

An eminent member of a family native to Elba, Giuseppe Tonietti would become the concession holder of the Elba iron mines in 1888. After his death in 1894, he was succeeded by his son Ugo Ubaldo Tonietti. Together with the director of the mining company, Pilade del Buono, the son would form a very enterprising partnership, establishing a blast-furnace plant at Portoferraio so that the iron ore mined on the island could be smelted locally. At the beginning of the 20th century the Tonietti family fortunes were at their high point. It was then that Ugo Ubaldo decided to have this mausoleum built at Cavo. Work on the monument began in 1904 and was completed two years later. It would never be used as a tomb because the family did not obtain permission for a private burial place.

SIGHTS NEARBY:

AN "IRON CROSS" OF PYRITES ❷

Alfeo Ricci Mineralogy Museum, Via Palestro 57031 Capoliveri (LI). Tel: 0565 93 54 92. Opening hours: from April to October, daily 10.00-13.00 and 16.30-18.30. Admission: 2.50 €, reduced: 1.50 €

The Elba Mineralogy Museum houses the important collection of minerals gathered together by its founder, Alfeo Ricci. One unusual piece is a double pentadodecahedron – that is, a sixty-sided piece – of iron pyrites in the form of an 'iron cross'. Composed primarily of sulphur and iron, pyrites is very common on Elba. It owes its name to the Greek for fire (pyros): when it is struck against iron, it sparks. The rarity of this particular piece is that the two crystals within the pyrites have grown across each other to form this strange motif of the "iron cross".

CASA SALDARINI

❸

Villini 1 Car Park
The Archaeological Park of Baratti and Populonia
Baratti
57025 Piombino (LI)

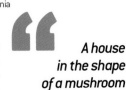

*A house
in the shape
of a mushroom*

This abandoned house in the middle of the Archaeology Park seems to have been entirely forgotten about ever since its construction in 1962 for the Saldarini family. Designed by the architect Vittorio Giorgini, it was inspired by the idea that architectural forms should echo those of the natural world and therefore fit in with the natural environment. This house was a first in Italy for both method of construction and the materials used. There were those who criticised it at the time as kitsch, as nothing but a piece of sculpture, or as a house without form. The nicknames given to the building – the "tortoise", the "elephant", etc – reveal the attempts made to identify the daring design with something familiar and obvious.

A little too avant-garde for its day, the house found no new buyer after the Saldarini family moved in the 1980s.

Another building by Vittorio Girogini stands not far away: the wood-built holiday home called L'Esagono [the Hexagon]. This is visible, from the outside only, if you take the path to the right that runs around Casa Saldarini. The concept behind this structure was modular, given that it consists of prefabricated hexagonal components (like those that make up a beehive), which were then fitted together and organised in accordance with the owner's requirements.

VITTORIO GIORGINI

Born in Florence in 1926, Vittorio Giorgini began teaching architecture in the United States in 1969. Most of the models and plans of the designs by this very atypical architect are now to be found in France (at the Centre Pompidou in Paris and the FRAC in Orléans) or in Switzerland (at the Vita Design Museum, Basle). Giorgini's works in Tuscany also include a school in Bibbona. Author of a number of books, the architect is known for his iconoclastic ideas. One of his works is available on-line for consultation at: www.bibliotecamarxista.org/autori/giorgini%20vittorio.htm

His architectural work is discussed in Marco Del Francia's *Vittorio Giorgini, la natura come modello* published by Edizioni Angelo Pontecorboli in 2000.

Directions: there are no signs indicating the Casa Saldarini. Take the SP23 which links San Vincenzo and Piombino and then follow the arrows to the Baratti and Populonia Archaeological Park. Turn right into the first car park (Villini 1) and leave your car at the end of the road, in the area of the bars and restaurants. Then take the beaten-earth track that starts to the left of the Demos restaurant, and walk for around one hundred metres. Casa Saldarini is within a walled garden and the gate is locked. The building is now abandoned and the garden overgrown (obstructing the view to the sea). Unfortunately it is not possible to visit the interior.

THE MYSTERIES OF CAMPIGLIA

Church of San Giovanni – Municipal Cemetery. Via di Venturina
57021 Campiglia Marittima (LI)
• Cemetery opening hours: from 1 May to 30 September 7.30-18.00 (Mondays and Fridays 17.00-18.00); 1 October to 30 April 8.00-17.00 (Mondays and Fridays from 14.00-17.00).
• "House of Alchemy". 4 Via B. Buozzi . 57021 Campiglia Marittima (LI)

*Perfect
for lovers of
the esoteric*

For lovers of the esoteric, the village of Campiglia Marittima is a little paradise; the streets in the village and the area around the church of San Giovanni are full of mysterious symbols and details.

The church walls have been roped off to prevent visitors getting too close, so you need binoculars to read a plaque with a palindrome identical to one that can be found in Siena:

SATOR
AREPO
TENET
OPERA
ROTAS

For the explanation, see the chapter on Siena (page 108).

A few metres away, the ground in front of the church door is paved with what was undoubtedly a tombstone. This bears various inscriptions - including one which reads Tolomeus Petri et Flore – and a very curious central motif: an androgynous body which is male below the waist, female above (the figure seems to be holding a torch in its right hand, while supporting itself against some sort of slanting board). Strangely, this same figure reappears on the house at number 4 Via B. Buozzi in the village. There it is more distinct and one can make out details that are not so clear on the church flagstone: for example, the figure's right hand no longer seems to be holding a torch but rather the number '3'. Surrounding the image one sees a number of esoteric symbols, which have inevitably led some to argue that this is a "House of Philosophy" associated with alchemy. Unfortunately there is no real explanation as to who the "philosopher" in question might be ... just as there is no explanation for the air of mystery with which the village seems to both excite and defeat curiosity.

Note: you have to walk through the cemetery to reach the church. The gate locks automatically at closing time (further adding to the air of mystery here). Thus you are strongly advised to respect the opening times if you do not want to end up locked in the cemetery overnight...

THE TRIPLE ENCLOSURE
OF SAN SILVESTRO CATHEDRAL

⑤

San Silvestro Park of Archaeology and Mining
34b,Via di San Vincenzo. 57021. Campiglia Marittima (LI)
• Tel: 0565 83 86 80 • Fax: 0565 83 87 03
• Guided tours and bookings: 0565 22 64 45
• E-Mail: parcoss@parchivaldicornia.it • www.parchivaldicornia.it
• Opening times: from June to September, Tuesday to Sunday; in July and August, daily; and from March to May, Saturdays, Sundays, and holidays. In winter you are advised to phone ahead to confirm. The park opens at 10am, and closes at different times according to the season of the year. Admission to the park, with all the various facilities (little train, museums, commentaries): 9 €, reduced: 5 €

Traditional game or esoteric symbol ?

The San Silvestro Citadel - the Rocca di San Silvestro – can be reached either on foot (a forty minute walk) or by means of the small train that carries guided tours and leaves at set times (every hour during high season).

The Citadel of San Silvestro dates from the year 1004. Near the fortified main gate is a curious motif carved into the stone (now protected by a glass panel). Not far away, another identical motif can be found on the third step of the entrance staircase; it is not signposted. A panel at the main way explains that the carving depicts the game of filetto [Nine Men's Morris] which was played by the guards here during the long hours when they were on watch.

Also known as "Merels", Nine Men's Morris is known to have been played in ancient Egypt, Greece and Rome. The motif of the morris board can be found in England (Whitby Abbey, Westminster Abbey, Canterbury Cathedral), in France (the Abbey of Chaalis, Oise) and at innumerable places in Italy: the castle of Campolattaro (Benevento, Campania), the basilica of St. John Lateran (Rome), the church of San Francesco in Alatri (outside Frosinone, Latium) and the church of San Rocco (Venice) ... to name but a few. The game was played on a board of three concentric squares; the centres of each side linked by a line, with diagonals also running from the corner of the inner square out to the corner of the outer. The resulting junctions of lines and square form the 24 places where the two players could, one at a time, put down their nine men (or pawns). The aim was to form a full line of three whilst preventing your opponent from doing the same. Sometimes the pieces were simply different-coloured pebbles.

Some have argued against this interpretation of the motif, saying that it actually depicts the esoteric symbol of the "triple enclosure"; the citadel of San Silvestro itself is in part contained within triple rings of ramparts. To support their theory they point out that the diagram is vertical, and therefore could not have been used to play Nine Men's Morris. Various explanations of the triple enclosure have been put forward. Some have said it is a ground plan of the city of Poseidon, the capital of Atlantis, some that it is a representation of the Temple of Jerusalem contained within its triple walls, and still others that it is a diagrammatic depiction of an alchemical "squaring of the circle."

Another game board was found during excavations at the citadel. This was used for the game of alquerque (el qirkat), which the Arabs had introduced into Spain some time around the 10th century.

PETRA AZIENDA AGRICOLA

131, San Lorenzo Alto. 57038 Suvereto (LI)
• Tel: 0565 84 53 08 • E-mail: info@petrawine.it • http://www.petrawine.it
• Visits and wine-tasting by appointment only.

A monument to architecture in the middle of the countryside

The first thought that comes to mind when you get to the Petra winery is that you have taken a wrong turn somewhere. It's easy to imagine that this spectacular building is a Futurist monument commemorating some extraordinary event., But much more prosaically, it is in fact the premises of the vineyards run by the father and daughter team of Vittorio and Francesca Moretti, who commissioned renowned architect Mario Botta to design the structure. The property covers some 300 hectares of vineyards, woods and olive groves, producing four different ranges of wines and olive oil (sold in a bottle also of very unusual design).

MARIO BOTTA
Born on 1 April 1943 at Mendrisio (in the Swiss canton of Ticino), Mario Botta is undoubtedly a leading figure in contemporary architecture. Having joined an architectural studio as a junior draughtsman at the age of 15, he would design his first building a year later: the presbytery at Genetrerio (Ticino). He would then take up his studies again and open his own studio in 1970 in Lugano. Since then he has produced work that exemplifies a personal style which he describes as embodying a "regressive utopia", and a "refuge centred once more upon tradition." His buildings show a marked preference for the use of brick, with designs often employing a keystone motif along with a massive central cylinder. His most famous projects include the cathedral at Ñvry (France), the San Francisco Museum of Modern Art (USA), the Gotardo Bank (Lugano, Switzerland), the extension and modernisation of La Scala Opera House in Milan (Italy) and, most famous of all, the "Round House" at Stabio (Switzerland).

SIGHTS NEARBY:
STATUE OF CARDUCCI'S GRANDMOTHER ❼
Piazza Alberto. Bolgheri. 57022 Castagneto Carducci (LI)
Alhough there is no sign recording the fact, the model for the statue of the old lady calmly sitting on a bench in the central square of this fine little village was in fact the grandmother of the Italian poet Giosuè Carducci. His beloved "Nonna Lucia" had a decisive influence on his early years, even though she died when he was seven years old. She is mentioned in a number of his works, most notably in Davanti San Guido. Born on 27 July 1835, Giosuè Carducci lived in Bolgheri until 1848 (his father was a doctor here). The poet would ultimately win the Nobel Prize for Literature in 1906, though he was too ill at the time to go and receive the award. He died on 16 February 1907 in Bologna.

THE MADONNA OF FRASSINE

The Frassine Sanctuary, 58020 Frassine (GR)
• Tel/Fax: 0566 91 00 00
• www.santuariomadonnadelfrassine.com
• Opening hours: daily, 8.45-12.00 and 14.00-17.00

> *A miraculous Madonna on a tree-trunk*

Standing in an illuminated niche above the high altar, the miraculous statue of the Madonna is immediately visible when you enter the church of the Sanctuary of Frassine. Access behind the altar is via the iron gates on either side (ask the priest or sacristan). Once there, you discover the apse of the small original chapel that has been incorporated within this larger church. Upon opening the door to the right of the apse you are greeted by an amazing sight: the tall trunk of an ash tree on which the statue of the Virgin stands.

In the 6th century St. Regulus, having fled Africa because of the persecution of the Christians, landed with several of his disciples at Baratta. All the saint brought with him was a cedar-wood statue of the Virgin, which would be preserved by the monks of the monastery of San Pietro near Monteverdi Marritimo after Regulus was beheaded by order of Totila, king of the Ostrogoths.

In the 13th century the monastery was sacked and destroyed. However, a monk by the name of Mariano managed to carry the statue to safety, hiding it within the branches of an ash tree. One century later, a herdsman was made curious by the fact that his animals always knelt down at one precise spot in the forest. Upon investigation, he found the statue, resting upon the trunk of the tree as upon a high pedestal. The statue was then carried to a local church, only to later return in some inexplicable manner to its place in the tree. Understanding the significance of this return, the local people built a chapel around the statue, and the sanctuary of Frassine subsequently became the site of numerous miracles.

EX-VOTOS AT THE SANCTUARY OF THE MADONNA ❾ OF MONTENERO

57128 Livorno (LI)
• Tel: 0586 57 771
• E-Mail: info@santuariomontenero.org • www.santuariomontenero.org
• Opening hours: Sundays and holidays 7.00-13.00 and 14.30-18.00; weekdays 7.30-12.30 and 14.30-18.30.

> *An ex-voto that inspired the plot of Rossini's opera, L' Italiana in Algeri*

L ocated in a spot overlooking Livorno and the surrounding area, the sanctuary of Montenero was built in 1721 on the site of a miracle. It contains a large number of ex-votos, most of them for grace received at sea. Alongside the naïve but moving paintings of shipwrecks and storms, there are also works of exceptional artistic quality, making the ex-votos here into a veritable museum collection of seascapes. However, the ex-votos are not always paintings. For example, there is the bloody undervest of a policeman (left in 1935), or the waistcoat and oriental slippers of a young woman from Ponsivinio who, around the year 1800, was seized by Turkish pirates while out strolling along the beach of Antignano. Taken to Constantinople, she was forced to enter the Sultan's harem. Then one day her incessant prayers to the Virgin were answered: there in the harem's garden she saw her own brother, who, with the Virgin's help, had come to rescue her. When she arrived back home, she had her Turkish clothes framed and then took them as an ex-voto to the Montenero sanctuary, where they can still be seen today.

Some say that it was this ex-voto which suggested the plot of Rossini's L'Italiana in Algeri, whilst others argue the story was based upon the misfortunes which befell the Milanese gentlewoman Antonietta Frapolli: captured by pirates, she was taken to Algiers and forced to become part of the harem of the Bey, but would eventually be brought back to Italy by a Venetian ship.

The church also has other "Islamic" ex-votos: to thank the Madonna of Montenero for the intercession which spared him the amputation of a wounded leg, the son of the Bey of Tunis sent the sanctuary a model of that same limb in solid silver.

EX-VOTOS
The term "ex-voto" is an abbreviated form of the Latin ex voto suscepto, meaning "by reason of the vow made". These are tokens of gratitude offered to a saint (or the Virgin Mary) after a "miracle" has occurred, very often involving survival of shipwreck, accident, or illness. When a saint has answered the prayers of the faithful, the ex-voto offered can take either the form of an object (such as a crutch or a lifebuoy) or, more often, a naïve but descriptive painting of the incident involved. Sometimes ex-votos can even be anthropomorphic (see page 132 in connection with the sanctuary of Romituzzo).

THE ENGLISH CEMETERY IN LIVORNO ❿

Misericordia di Livorno
63, Via Giuseppe Verdi. 57126 Livorno (LI)
• Tel: 0586 89 73 24
• Ask for the keys at the office of the Misericordia di Livorno
• Opening hours: Monday to Thursday 9.00-12.00 and 14.00-17.00,
Friday 9.00-12.00.

Italy's oldest Protestant cemetery

The English cemetery of Livorno is a very unexpected and secluded spot in the centre of the city. Visited by scholars, curious English tourists, and those devoted to St. Elizabeth Seaton (see below), it is a charming place where the shrubs and plants have gradually reasserted their rights, in some cases overturning the tombstones. Amidst birdsong, buzzing insects, and occasionally, the strident sound of televisions in the nearby apartment blocks, one has to step carefully to avoid tripping over the overgrown stones that litter the ground. Sometimes the eye is caught by a Swiss tombstone, for although this place is referred to as the "English Cemetery", it was used by all those of Protestant faith, irrespective of nationality. However, it is the United Kingdom which, via its Consulate in Florence, remains responsible for this "little corner of Britain." Until 1827, when the Swiss Reformed Church opened an ecumenical cemetery in Florence, all foreigners who died in Italy and were neither Catholic nor Jewish could only be buried here at Livorno (or Leghorn, as the English called it at the time).

The dates on the tombstones reveal a curious paradox: the cemetery was in use long before it was officially recognised. In fact, that official recognition only came in 1746, while the oldest tombstone here dates back to 1594. The cemetery would remain in use until 1839, when a new one was opened near the city's San Marco gate. Protected by a sheet of glass, the most frequently visited tomb here is that of William Magee Seaton, husband of St. Elizabeth Seaton, who was herself converted to Catholicism while living in Livorno. Paul Valéry compared the English cemetery in Livorno to a sculptor's studio.

SAINT ELIZABETH ANN SEATON

Born in New York City on 28 August 1774 into a Protestant family, Ann Bayley would marry William Magee Seaton in 1794. After her husband went bankrupt and then fell ill with TB, the family travelled to Livorno in the hope that the sea air might provide a cure. However, William faded fast and would be buried in the English cemetery.

Elisabeth, by now a convert to Catholicism, returned to the USA with her five children and became a teacher. She would open a school for young girls in Maryland, then a religious community – the Sisters of Charity – in Baltimore. She died on 4 January 1821 and was canonised on 14 September 1975 by Pope Paul VI. She was the first woman in the United States to be declared a saint.

SIGHTS NEARBY:

THE MARBLE BRIDGE **11**

The bridge which links Via Borra and Via Porticciolo owes its name to the marble edging on which numerous boatmen and porters have, over the decades, engraved names and inscriptions. These commemorations of dead friends, sometimes referred to solely by their surname, are often very moving. For example, one reads: "To the dear memory of Giovanni Calafatti who ceased to enjoy the gentle breeze of life on 16 September 1854, at the age of 26, being carried off by an evil sickness. His friends in condolence for such a loss had this marble carved. P.P. [Pregate per Lui. Pray for Him]"

RUINS OF THE MAUSOLEUM OF COSTANZO CIANO **12**

Monte Burrone. 57128 Livorno (LI)

The mausoleum can be reached by car or on foot (600 metres from the car park). From the car park for the Montenero sanctuary, take Via Giovanni XXIII and then turn left into the first unsurfaced road, Viale Tirreno.

At the top of Monte Burrone stands a massive square tower now heavily tagged by graffiti artists and in the process of being reclaimed by nature. This is all that is left of the unfinished mausoleum of Costanzo Ciano, father of Galeazzo Ciano, who was Benito Mussolini's son-in-law (husband of his daughter Edda) and Foreign Minister in the Fascist government. Famous for a feat of arms carried out in 1918 – by boat, he managed to penetrate 80 km behind the Austrian defences at Buccari in Croatia – Costanzo Ciano was honoured by Mussolini with this monumental mausoleum, designed by the architect Arturo Dazzi, a personal friend of Galeazzo Ciano. But dismayed by his country's adverse fortunes during the Second World War, Galeazzo attempted to negotiate a separate peace for Italy with the Allies in 1943. Arrested by the Nazis, he was handed over to Mussolini, who had him shot on 11 January 1944... Hence the mausoleum to his father was never finished...

THE FIRST APARTMENT BLOCKS IN ITALY - VENEZIA NUOVA DISTRICT **13**

Begun in the 17th century, work on the New Venice district produced Italy's first apartment blocks. These collective residential buildings, with different apartments on different floors, were intended to provide those who worked at sea with functional accommodation near the port. Most of the structures were destroyed by Allied bombing in 1944, but they were later rebuilt exactly as they had been.

PALAZZO GAUDI **14**

Via della Repubblica. 57013 Rosignano Solvay (LI)

Loosely inspired by the style of Gaudi, this building proudly asserts its links with that architect's work. Designed by Veronica Cantina, it has provoked very varied reactions amongst the inhabitants of Rosignano. The structure certainly stands out amidst the usual urban fabric and all of its apartments were quickly sold, confirming the success of this original project. The architect dedicated one of the main entrance towers to the Sun and the other to the Moon.

Piazza della Repubblica – The Widest Bridge in Europe

Built in 1844 to join the old and new districts of the city, Piazza della Repubblica is in effect a bridge spanning the city's main canal, the Fosse Reale. 240 metres in width, it is therefore – as the guidebooks point out – the widest bridge in Europe.

GROSSETO
AND SURROUNDINGS

THE TOMB OF TIBURZI, THE "BANDIT KING" ❶

Capalbio Cemetery
Via Giacomo Leopardi
58011 Capalbio (GR)

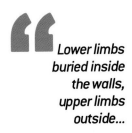

Lower limbs buried inside the walls, upper limbs outside...

In the period immediately before the Unification of Italy the poorest peasants survived only thanks to such time-honoured rights as riverside fishing, the collection of windfall timber and the gleaning of cornfields. The abolition of these rights meant penury for hundreds, with some being forced to become bandits and outlaws if they were not to starve. Domenico Tiburzi, known as Domenichino, was one such. Born at Cellere (outside Viterbo) on 26 May 1836, he was the most famous of all the bandits in the area, actually being nicknamed "The King of Maremma". He drew a distinction between justice and the written law, and owed his popularity to his observance of a personal moral code: for example, he robbed from the rich to give to the poor, and once killed a fellow bandit who was "doing wrong." But he was also accused of working as "'muscle'" for a number of rich landowners, carrying out well-paid "contracts" that were not inspired by any fine sense of justice.

Eventually, in 1896, Tiburzi was ambushed and shot by the carabinieri, just outside Capalbio; the famous picture of the bandit leaning against a column in the Capalbio cemetery is actually a photograph of his dead body held in place by ropes. Initially, the Church refused to accede to the popular demand that the bandit be given a religious burial. Finally, a compromise was reached and Tiburzi was buried under the very wall of the cemetery, with this lower limbs reaching into sacred ground, but the upper part of his body lying outside. Today there is no gravestone to mark the tomb; but one can still see the column that appears in the famous photograph. A small wooden panel recalls the date and place of Tiburzi's death.

If you want to know more, go to the Trattoria Da Maria in the village, where there is an exhibit of newspaper articles and other documents dealing with the life and beaux gestes of Domenico Tiburzi.
Trattoria Da Maria, 3 Via Comunale - 58011 Capalbio (GR). Tel: 0564 89 60 14.
Closed Tuesdays and from 7 January to 10 February.
Tiburzi, Paolo Benvenuti's film about the bandit, came out in 1996.

For lovers of stories of brigands and bandits, there is also the opportunity to sleep in the house that once belonged to the famous bandit Antonio Magrini, nicknamed "Il Basilocco'". The last great brigand of the Maremma, he was killed by the carabinieri in 1904. The weapons he had with him at his death – a pistol, a rifle and a dagger – have been preserved.
Fattoria di Peruzzo 58028 Roccatederighi (GR). Tel: 0564 56 98 73. E-mail: info@peruzzofattoria.com. www.peruzzofattoria.com. From 420? to 670? per week.

THE TAROT GARDEN

Garavicchio. 58011 Capalbio (GR)
• Tel: 0564 89 51 22 • E-mail: tarotg@tin.it • www.nikidesaintphalle.com
• Opening hours: 1 April to 15 October 14.30-19.30. November to March, open free of charge (by explicit request of Niki de Saint Phalle) on the first Saturday of each month, 9.00-13.00.
• Admission: 10,50 ?, reduced: 6 €.

A fascinating journey within the esoteric world of Niki de Saint-Phalle

The inspiration for Niki de Saint Phalle's Tarot Garden came from youthful visits to Gaudi's Parco Güell in Barcelona and the Parco dei Mostri at Bomarzi (outside Viterbo).

Begun in 1979 and opened to the public in 1998, the immense garden contains giant statues (some more than 15 metres high) that represent the 22 "major arcana" of the Tarot pack. The body of these statues is made of reinforced concrete and polyester, using elaborate procedures that make them resistant to earthquakes; their surface is covered with mosaics of Murano glass, ceramics and mirrors. During the long period she was working on this project, the artist actually lived within the Empress arcana (in the form of a sphinx), where one can still see a magnificent sitting-room, a bathroom and a small bedroom.

In conformity with the artist's wish that each person should experience the garden in their own personal way, there are no guided tours. But you can obtain a leaflet which, while not providing explanatory comments as such, does contain hints by the artist as to how the entire project might be read. "The Tarot Garden," she writes, "is not only my garden; it belongs to all those who helped me produce it. I am the Architect of this garden. I imposed my vision because I could not do otherwise. This garden is the result of difficulties overcome by means of love, wild enthusiasm, obsession… and, above all, by faith, lots of faith. Nothing could have stopped me. As happens in all fairy stories, my route to the treasure brought me into contact with dragons, sorcerers, magicians and the Angel of Temperance."

NIKI DE SAINT-PHALLE

Catherine Marie-Agnès Fal de Saint-Phalle, known as Niki de Saint Phalle, was born in Neuilly-sur-Seine on 29 October 1930. Her family subsequently moved to the USA, where she would work first as a fashion model, then, from 1952 onwards, as a painter, becoming part of the New Realist group. She first became widely known for "Shootings", in which spectators participated in the creation of works by shooting at balloons of paint that then splattered plaster sculptures. She was also renowned for her "Nanas", brightly-coloured figures of buxom women. From 1979 onwards she would dedicate herself to the creation of her masterpiece, the Tarot Garden. She died in San Diego on 21 May 2002 as the result of a respiratory infection caused by the toxic vapours which, over the years, she had inhaled while working on her sculptures.

THE "CUT"

3

Ansedonia
58010 Orbetello (GR)
• Directions: Travelling southbound on the Via Aurelia, take the second exit (Ansedonia); travelling northbound it's the first exit. The road then takes you directly to the promontory.

A spectacular Roman canal cut into the rock

La Tagliata [The Cut] is a spectacular piece of Roman engineering dating from the 2nd century BC. Slicing through an 80-metre stretch of rock that is at times 20 metres deep, the canal was cut to link the Etruscan port of Cosa with the lake of Burano; it also served as a means of tidal control to prevent the port from silting up. Today, La Tagliata is freely open to visitors, a few minor adjustments having been made so that the entire site is accessible.

The Torre della Tagliata is a tower that was subsequently converted into a house. One famous resident was Giacomo Puccini, who lived here while working on Turandot, the opera he left unfinished at his death.

SIGHTS NEARBY:

TRANSATLANTIC HYDROPLANE FLIGHTS FROM ORTEBELLO AIR BASE ❹

Parco delle Crociere. 1-7, Via Marconi, 58010 Orbetello (GR)

The monument is protected by a gate, but those in charge are quite happy to open it for visitors. If no one is around, contact: Air Force Captain Romualdi: 329 36 08 085, Mr. Giusti Alfredo: 0564 86 76 13, Command Post, Air Force Deposit 64b, Porto Santo Stefano: 0564 81 68 02

The Parco delle Crociere stands on the site of the Orbetello Air Base, destroyed by the Germans in 1944. A monument recalls that this airfield was the starting-point for a number of legendary flights, two of them undertaken by Italo Balbo (see below). What was so spectacular about these flights was that they involved a large number of hydroplanes and covered distances that were remarkable for the time. The first of these took place in 1928, with more than 60 hydroplanes crossing the western Mediterranean, from Orbetello to Los Alcazares in Spain. Italo Balbo would later pilot two transatlantic flights – to Rio de Janeiro (1930) and New York and Chicago (1933). These flights attracted huge international media coverage, promoting a very positive and modern image of Italy.

ITALO BALBO

Italo Balbo was born near Ferrara on 6 June 1896. Although the son of a bourgeois family which supported the monarchy, as a young man he made his political commitment to republican ideas known. After earning medals and promotion to the rank of captain during the First World War, Balbo became a member of the Fascist movement, and was one of the four main figures in the "March on Rome" in 1922. Quick to brawl with Communists and Socialists, he was even accused of the murder of an anti-Fascist priest. But the Ferrara court which reheard the case in 1947, after the collapse of Fascism, would exonerate him.

Balbo's passion for flying led to his appointment as Minister of Aviation at the age of 33, making him the youngest government minister in Europe. It was while he held that position that he would undertake his two famous transatlantic flights (see above). His fame was then at its height: streets in America were named after him; New York gave him a ticker-tape parade; the Sioux named him "Chief Flying Eagle" and in common parlance the word "balbo" was used to refer to a fleet of aircraft.

Becoming Governor of Libya in 1934, he would initiate various grandiose projects, including the coastal road that became known as Via Balbia. In 1939, the Nazi invasion of Poland brought to a head the decline in his relationship with Mussolini, whom he criticised for his alliance with the Germans and for the promulgation of the Race Laws. On 28 June 1940, Balbo's plane was shot down by Italian anti-aircraft guns when he was returning from a reconnaissance flight over Tobruk. Certain people, including his widow, cast doubt on the official version of events, claiming he had been murdered on Mussolini's orders. In fact, Mussolini himself once said that Balbo was the only man he feared, because he thought that Balbo alone was capable of assassinating him.

The day after Balbo's death, a Royal Air Force plane piloted by Raymond Collishaw, a Canadian air ace during the First World War, flew over the Italian military camp to drop a wreath with a sash expressing the RAF's condolences. Along with those of his crew members, Italo Balbo's tomb can be seen in the Orbetello cemetery, in Viale Donatori del Sangue.

STATUE OF CARAVAGGIO

❺

Braccio Car Park
La Feniglia Beach
Porto Ercole
58019 Monte Argentario (GR)
Parking: 1 € an hour

> *Beneath the sands of La Feniglia lies the body of Caravaggio...*

A mong the various aspects of Caravaggio's life that are shrouded in mystery, his birth and death continue to puzzle scholars. While we know that the painter – real name, Michelangelo Merisi – was born on 29 September 1571, it has yet to be established with certainty that his birthplace actually was Caravaggio, just outside Bergamo. Some biographers argue that he was born in Milan and that he then spent part of his childhood in the village which would give him his artistic name. As for his death, it raises a number of unanswered questions. We know that the artist was sentenced to death for having killed a certain Ranuccio Tommasoni in a duel. As a result he was forced to live outside Rome. Later, after hearing that the Pope was going to grant him a pardon, he tried to return to the city by sea. However, when his ship put in at Porto Ercole (or, as some argue, Palo, near the Etruscan necropolis of Cerveteri), he is said to have been arrested by customs officers but then released upon payment of a ransom. By the time he got free, the boat carrying his baggage and paintings he intended to present to the Pope had left port. And in his frantic efforts to beat it to its next port of call, Caravaggio is said to have caught a fever on the deserted beach of La Feniglia, dying on 18 July 1610. But there are also those who claim that he was the victim of a hired killer…

While his actual burial place has never been found, in 2001 scholars did unearth the record of his death in the parish register of the church of Sant-Erasmo in Porto Ercole. Ironically, the artist died without knowing that the Pope had put his seal to the act of pardon…

Directions: From Orbetello take the road to Porto Ercole, then turn left towards Ansedonia. Turn left again at the sign reading Parking, noleggio bici, spiaggia libera [car park, bike hire, and public beach]. There are no signposts to the monument, so the best thing to do is park at the Braccio car park, then take the wide beaten-earth track that continues on from the side opposite the car park entrance; a milestone there reads 0 km on one side, 6 km on the other. Almost immediately to the left is an unmarked but clearly well-trodden path through the pine trees. This will bring you to another beaten-earth track that runs parallel to the first. Turn left into this, and the monument is about 100 metres further on. If you have doubts, ask the car park attendant or one of the numerous senior citizens who cycle along these paths.

MOSAICS IN THE CHURCH
OF SANTISSIMA TRINITÀ

6

Via Ss Trinità
Pozzarello
Porto Santo Stefano
58019 Monte Argentario (GR)

The "Two Europes" joined under the Trinity

The church of Santa Trinità was consecrated in 2002. The first thing that strikes you upon entering is the large mosaic covering the apse wall behind the high altar. These aesthetically daring motifs and colours are unusual, even for a modern church, and are the work of a team from the Ezio Aletti Centro Studi e Ricerche.

With its head office in Rome, the Aletti Centre was set up by the Jesuits to further mutual understanding between the "two Europes" that are in the process of political unification. Specialists in the culture and religion of central and eastern Europe, members of the Centre work to promote cultural exchange and cooperation. While spiritual questions are an essential concern for the centre, it also collaborates in the decoration of new places of worship, drawing upon such traditional artistic crafts as mosaics.

The work in the church of Santa Trinità depicts the Holy Trinity, with the hand of God the Father above and the dove which symbolises the Holy Spirit. Below is the third member of the Trinity, Jesus, who reaches out towards Adam and Eve. The figure of the pelican was a traditional symbol of sacrifice: it was once believed that the bird pecked its chest so that its offspring could drink its blood.

CENTRO STUDI E RICERCHE EZIO ALETTI
25, Via Paolina. 00184 Rome
Tel: 06 48 24 588 - Fax: 06 48 58 76
http://www.centroaletti.com
Pozarello lies between Orbetello and Porto Santo Stefano. The road up to the church (Via Ss Trinità) runs off the main street. The church bell-tower provides a clear visual landmark.

THE MADONNA OF THE CAT FLAP

❼

Church of San Giorgio
Piazza San Giorgio
58014 Montemerano (GR)

> *A 15th century painting... complete with cat flap*

The church of San Giorgio at Montemerano is known best for a polyptych by Sano di Pietro (1406-1481), The Madonna and Child with Saints. But to the right of the high altar is another painting that is worthy of attention. Now known as "La Madonna della gattaiola" [Madonna of the Cat Flap], this wood panel was painted around 1450 by a pupil of Sassetta's (1392-1451) who would become known as Il Maestro di Montemerano. Originally, it was part of a diptych of The Annunciation. However, when the door to the cellar in the presbytery broke, the parish priest decided to replace it with this panel, which happened to be the same size. The problem was that he kept salami, cheese and fruit in his cellar, so he needed a cat down there to keep off the rats and mice. To make it possible for this feline guard to come and go, he had a round hole cut in the panel. It is still there, perfectly visible, and has given the work its present nickname.

SIGHTS NEARBY:

A RARE IMAGE OF THE LEGENDARY BAPHOMET

❽

Parish Church of Santa Cristina, Ospedaletto. 10, Viccolo III° Borgo.
Rocchette di Fazio. 58055 Semproniano (GR)

The Templars' Cross on the pediment of the parish church of Santa Cristina at Roccchette di Fazio probably indicates that the church was once connected with the Knights Templar. Some claim that one of the knights is buried in the crypt, along with his horse, sword, and substantial treasure. Just alongside the church is the Ospedaletto, a small hospice for the pilgrims which dates from the 14th century: High up on the left side wall is a sculpture which is supposed to be a depiction of the legendary Baphomet, a figure who played a key role in the destruction of the Order of the Knights Templar.

BAPHOMET

The Baphomet is an idol which is sometimes depicted with two or three faces (generally bearded), and sometimes takes a more animal form. During their trial, the Knights Templar were accused of bowing in veneration before an image of Baphomet during their initiation rituals; hence the accusation of heresy levelled against them. Various theories have been put forward as to the origin of the name, one pointing out that in the langue d'oc spoken in southern France "Baphomet" is the distorted version of "Mohammed".

THE TOWER OF DAVID

❾

Monte Labro
58031 Arcidosso (GR
• Directions: Leave Arcidosso by the Strada del Monte Amiata (the SP 160). About 6km in the direction of Triana, there is a sign on the right to Monte Labro. Take this road, which after 3km brings you to a car park and a small chalet for visitors (open during the tourist season). Allow a good 15 minutes for the walk to the top of the hill.

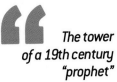

The tower of a 19th century "prophet"

«**G**iurisdavidism» was a 19th century movement named after its founder, David Lazzaretti. In 1868 he and his disciples raised this tower on an area of bare rock exposed to the elements; the wind here can sometimes be very strong. The view from the top of the tower (altitude: 1,193m) is quite simply exceptional. The entrance to the tower itself is in the unusual form of an inverted "V". If you have brought a torch with you, it is also possible to explore the underground area, whose entrance is immediately below the tower; the grill is closed only to keep out animals. Once inside, you can see the (now empty) chapel where the faithful used to meet.

The Centro Studi Lazzaretti in Arcidosso has various mementoes of Lazzaretti's life as well as all the documentation relating to Giurisdavidism, a utopian socio-religious movement.

DAVID LAZARETTI

Born in Arcidosso in 1834, David Lazzaretto had his first visions when suffering from an attack of malaria. The young man then abandoned his wife and children to join the army. Having returned, he was one day at the top of Monte Labro when the Virgin appeared to him, announcing that he was descended from the House of Capet and that he had an evangelical mission to fulfil. Opinion varies as to whether the man was a prophet, a magus, or the leader of a sect. What is true is that his "New Zion" attracted an increasing number of followers. Preaching a sort of utopian-mystical socialism, Davide Lazzaretti would fall foul of the Catholic Church, which excommunicated him and forbade him all religious office. The authorities, too, took an increasingly repressive attitude and Lazzaretti himself would be shot dead by the police in Arcidosso while leading a demonstration on 18 August 1878. His body would later be exhumed and handed over to the (in)famous anthropologist Cesare Lombroso, the founder of morphopsychology and advocate of the theory of the "born criminal".

CENTRO STUDI LAZZARETTI. 30, Piazza Indipendenza. 58031 Arcidosso (GR)
• Tel: 0564 966438 • E-mail biblioteca@amiata.net
• www.centrostudilazzaretti.it

THE CROSSES OF BALDASSARE AUDIBERT 🔟

Around Castel del Piano (GR)

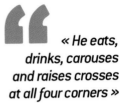

« He eats, drinks, carouses and raises crosses at all four corners »

At the middle of the 19th century a very strange fellow came to live in Castel del Piano. Was Baldassare Audibert, a guest of the owners of Palazzo Ginanneschi (today the Town Hall), actually a French bishop, a Belgian-born officer in Napoleon's armies, or simply a Frenchman from Vercelli in Piedmont?

What we do know is that, after a pilgrimage to Rome, he began raising crosses all over the locality of Castel del Piano, saying that he did so as an act of penitence for the fact that, as a member of the Convention during the French Revolution, he had voted for the execution of both Louis XVI and Marie-Antoinette.

The local people do not seem to have taken him that seriously, as one can see from this mocking verse:

Baldassarre Audiberte
Mangia beve e si diverte
Pianta croci alli cantoni
Alla barba dei coglioni*

Sixteen of these crosses can now be seen in Castel del Piano and the neighbouring towns. Some were restored recently; others were changed in the past by having the original wood replaced by iron. The base of each cross is generally a hemisphere of stone bearing the initials B.A.P. (Baldassare Audibert Pax), with the date of the year the cross was raised (usually 1846).

DIRECTIONS TO TWO OF THE AUDIBERT CROSSES:
The Federico Cross
This wooden cross stands on the national highway (SS 323) running towards Monte Amiata, near the Castel del Piano exit and at the crossroads with the road on the right to Colle Vergari. Note the lilies at the top of the cross and at the end of the horizontal beam. A face is depicted at the centre. On the base is the usual inscription: "B.A.P. 1846".
The Colle Vergari Cross
At the crossroads marked by the Federico Cross (see above), take the road to Colle Vergari. The road runs round the village, and the cross stands where it doubles back towards the houses. The original wood cross has been replaced by one in iron.

A complete list of the crosses – with map and photos – can be found on the Internet: www.progettoamiataimmagini.com/croci.html

---

* "Baldassarre Audiberte
Eats, drinks and carouses
Raising crosses at ever corner,
Whatever dickheads might think"

THE GARDEN OF DANIEL SPOERRI

❶

58038 Seggiano (GR)
• Tel: 0564 950 805
• E-mail: ilgiardino@ilsilene.it
• http://www.danielspoerri.org/
• Il Silene Restaurant
• Opening hours: from Easter to 1 July, Tuesday to Sunday 11.00-20.00; 1 July to 15 September, daily 11.00-20.00; 15 September to 31October, Tuesday to Sunday 11.00-19.00; and from November to the end of March, by reservation only.
• Admission: 10 €. Students and children: 8 €.
Children under 8 years old: free admission

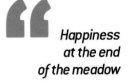

Happiness at the end of the meadow

Daniel Spoerri's garden is an extraordinary place. Created by the founder of the "New Realist" movement, the garden was opened in 1997 and provides a remarkable setting for around 100 works by more than 40 contemporary artists. Apart from the eyesore of overhead power cables, these sculptures, objects and installations are surrounded by unspoilt nature. When the gates open in the morning, the first visitors catch glimpses of rabbits, deer and squirrels scampering in the midst of these unusual works. Daniel Spoerri's aim was in fact to use the gentle Tuscan landscape to provide a natural backdrop for the art.

One such piece, by an artist who signs his work as "Not Vital", seems to show a man floating in the air against the façade of a building. What is most surprising, however, is how the area is "occupied" by figures that are apparently engaged in ordinary activities such as reading, knitting, or simply observing others.

It is a splendid experience. And a must for children, who will long remember their time spent in a garden totally given over to a sense of play.

THE REBUS OF THE CATHEDRAL

Cathedral of San Lorenzo
Piazza del Duomo
58100 Grosseto (GR)

On the façade of the cathedral of San Lorenzo in Grosseto there is a mysterious carving of a circle containing a rebus of initials. The solution in Latin reads *Soxus Rustichini Construxit Tempore Malavoltae Potestatis Roseti*, which can be translated as "Constructed by Sozzo Rustichini at the time of the Rule of Malavolti". It is simply the clever signature of the cathedral's builder.

> *A signature in the form of a rebus*

SIGHTS NEARBY:

ETRUSCAN BOWL IN THE MAREMMA ARCHAEOLOGICAL MUSEUM

3, Piazza Baccarini. 58100 Grosseto (GR)

• Tel: 0564 48 87 50 • E-mail: maam@gol.grosseto.it

• Opening hours: from 1 November to 28 February, Tuesday to Friday 9.00-13.00, Saturday and Sunday 9.30-13.00 and 16.30-19.00; 1 March to 30 April, Tuesday to Sunday 9.30-13.00 and 16.30-19.00; and 2 May to 31 October, Tuesday to Sunday 10.00-13.00 and 17.00-20.00.

• Admission: 5 €.

In the first display case to your right as you enter the first room (Sala 1), there is one of the most remarkable objects in the museum's Etruscan collection: a black terracotta bowl (*bucchero nero*) inscribed with the Etruscan alphabet. Dating from the 6th century BC, it has belonged to the museum since 1875, although its origin is unclear. Did it come from the ruins of Roselle, an Etruscan city located near the modern-day Grosseto, or from southern Etruria? It was not unusual for household objects to be decorated with the alphabet. We know that the Etruscans were a very literate people and therefore such objects were *aides mémoire* constantly available for consultation.

THE MYSTERY OF THE ETRUSCAN LANGUAGE

While the Etruscan alphabet has been known for some time, the language itself still remains partially shrouded in mystery. Experts have translated about 20,000 inscriptions, most of them short and repetitive phrases that appear on funeral monuments. This work was facilitated by the discovery in 1964 of the "Pyrgi Plates" (Pyrgi was one of the ports of the Etruscan city of Caere, the modern-day Cerveteri); two of these three gold plates bore the same text in Etruscan and Phoenician. But the entirety of known Etruscan texts has yet to be translated. One of the main difficulties scholars face is that the language is an "isolated" one — that is, it is not part of any known linguistic group.

SIGHTS NEARBY:

THE CHURCH OF THE SACRA FAMIGLIA

Complete with a cupola and a bell tower that looks very like a minaret, this remarkable church inevitably reminds one of a mosque. However, the cross atop both dome and tower leave one in no doubt as to which faith worships here. Built at the behest of the bishop of Grosseto, Monsignor Adelmo Tacconi, to serve the parish of new housing areas to the north of Grosseto, the Church of the Holy Family was designed by Enzo Pisaneschi and consecrated on 9 April 1989.

GROSSETO TIME PLAQUE

The Cathedral Bell Tower

Piazza Innocenzo II

Under an oculus of the bell tower is a small plaque that indicates the difference in real time between Rome (that is, at the cupola of St. Peter's) and this town. As a matter of fact, when it is exactly midday in Rome, it is only 11.54 and 39 seconds in Grosseto (see "Local Time" and "The Equation of Time" in Lucca, page 183).

OLD PUBLIC HYGIENE NOTICES

1, Via Ricasoli, also no. 1 and between nos. 2 and 4 Via Manin

In Grosseto there are notices announcing which days the streets are cleaned; any car found parked on that day is subject to a fine. This well-organised system of public hygiene is not a new thing in the town, as one can see from various marble plaques in its streets that used to announce the day on which the district was to be swept (failure to do so incurring a fine of one scudo) and the day when the "garbage" cart passed through the district. These undated plaques survive from the time when the town was divided into three distinct thirds, with clear demarcations of streets and the areas of business.

TELEGRAPH OFFICE ON THE GARIBALDI RAMPARTS

The kiosk is right on the Garibaldi Ramparts, next to the Eden Bar (at present a discothèque).

Curiously, the Central Telegraph Office in Grosseto has remained practically unchanged. Built in 1932-33, however, it has fallen victim to advances in telecommunications technology and is now disused. A recent fire in the dustbins stored against its wall caused some damage, but the cable panels with their old glass insulators still remain. The Central Office served Grosseto and the surrounding area, permitting the local population to send and receive important news.

GUILLOTINE IN THE ILDEBRANDO IMBERCIADORI LOCAL HISTORY MUSEUM ⑱

Via Ugurgeri 58030 Montepescali (GR)
• Contact: Signor Castellani at 0564 32 91 40 (evenings only)
• Opening hours: Wednesday to Sunday 15.00-18.30.

The last guillotine in Italy

Nicknamed the "Balcony of the Maremma", the village of Montepescali has a small local museum with numerous artefacts relating to local history: Etruscan and Roman pottery, old farming tools and implements, and archive documents providing details of the village's past. One of the main attractions is a clock mechanism that was stolen by Charles V's lansquenet mercenaries in 1555 and then rediscovered by chance in 1978 in the storerooms of the Museum of Geneva. But the most unusual exhibit here is a reconstruction

of a guillotine, which commemorates the village's connection with the last time such a machine was used in Grosseto: the victims were five bandits who, for a mere loaf of bread, had massacred the members of the Tacchia family in the Montepescali woods. Their execution took place on 18 November 1822.

The last execution by guillotine in Italy took place in Lucca on 29 July 1845, when five members of a band of brigands who had been terrorising the surrounding countryside were beheaded at the Porta San Donato. In 1847 the people of Lucca would actually hurl the blade of that guillotine into the sea at Viareggio, after setting fire to the wooden scaffold.

INSCRIPTIONS ON THE TORRE CANDELIERE ⑲

Torre del Candeliere. Piazza Matteotti
58024 Massa Marittima (GR)
• Tel: 0566 90 22 89
• E-mail: info@coopcollinemetallifere.it
The names carved on the outside of the tower can be seen from the street in Piazza Matteotti
• To visit the inside of the tower:
• Opening hours: from April to October, 10.00-13.00 and from 15.00-18.00; November to -March, 11.00-13.00 and 14.30-16.30. Closed Monday.
• Admission: 2.50 €.

Names of traitors inscribed in stone

Raised to assert the autonomy of the free commune of Massa Marittima in 1228, the Torre del Candeliere was a powerful local symbol – so much so that when the Sienese captured the town in 1333 they had two-thirds of it demolished in order to humble the vanquished population. As a result, the tower, which once stood 74 metres tall, now only rises 24 metres. The Sienese occupiers would, however, build the elegant arch that links the tower to the ramparts, and reorganise the fortifications of the citadel. Their main concern in doing so was not attack from outside but rather the threat posed by local uprisings. The inscriptions on the tower's stones are not immediately legible. One of them is in Latin and records the construction of the original tower in 1228, when Tedice Malabarba of Pisa was podestà. According to legend, the other inscription lists the traitors who helped the Sienese to take and sack the town in 1331. Certain historians support this claim, but a more likely theory is that the inscription gives the names of the assize court judge, Uberto Faselus, and the town camerario*(a certain Mellone) at the time the tower was originally built.

* The camerario - or chamberlain - was responsible for the 'chamber' of a religious or political ruler. The term "chamber" here is used to cover all aspects of the figure's private life – primarily, the management of his financial interests. In the Catholic Church, the camerario apostolico is responsible for the running of the pope's personal household.

THE SPRING OF ABUNDANCE AND THE TREE OF FECUNDITY ❷⓪

Piazzale Mazzini
58024 Massa Marittima (GR)
• Note: the fresco is undergoing restoration and, at the time of printing, was still not open to the public.

Dozens of male members in a 13th century fresco

The fresco within the porch containing the fountain in Piazza Mazzini will surprise even the most blasé hunters after the curious and bizarre. Painted in 1265 – the same year in which the fountain came into use – it depicts a tree bearing heavy fruit which, upon close inspection, turns out to be penises. The women standing beneath the laden branches are busy plucking the fruit and placing them in their baskets. Clearly allegorical in attention, this fresco is nevertheless very forthright in its realism – and demonstrates that religious subjects were not the only thing which attracted 13th century artists.

The fresco was only recently rediscovered after have lain for years "protected" by the thick layer of lime scale deposited by the water from the fountain – in fact , it had been effectively protected not only from the elements but also from the narrow-mindedness of those who would have been quick to censure such unorthodox work. Paradoxically, the removal of the lime scale damaged the fresco, so now the restoration has had to be reassessed by the Officio delle Pietri Dure in Florence. Hence the delay in the conclusion of work which, according to original estimates, should have been completed in 2005.

The name "Fountain of Abundance" does not allude to the copious flow of water but to the fact that the space above the arcade was given over to the storage of grain for use during periods of famine.

Photograph courtesy
of the Musei di Massa Marittima

AREZZO AND SURROUNDINGS

BOXES

FONDAZIONE ARCHIVIO DIARISTICO NAZIONALE-ONLUS

❶

Piazza Plinio Pellegrini, 1
52036 Pieve San Stefano (AR)
• Tel: 0575 79 77 30 – 31
• Fax: 0575 79 98 10
• E-mail: adn@archividiari.it • www.archividiari.it
• Opening hours: Monday to Friday 8.30-13.30 and 15.00-18.00. Saturdays 8.30-12.30.

Have your diary archived

The original idea came from journalist and writer Saverio Tutino: in 1984 he founded this archive of Italian personal diaries, as well as the Pieve-Banca Toscana prize for the most interesting examples of this particular form of writing. Advertised without great fanfare in a few national newspapers, the competition was a success from the start, with more than a hundred diaries submitted in its first year. Today this memory bank, which the organisers prefer to refer to as a 'seedbed', has become an important and well-established resource: the Fondazione Archivio Diaristico Nazionale–onlus.

Was it the fact that the town centre here was razed to the ground by the Nazis in 1944 that made Pieve Santo Stefano particularly sensitive to the question of historical memory? Perhaps. But whatever the reason, it is true that every year the Pieve collection acquires about 150 personal diaries, autobiographies or collections of letters, with the Archives now holding more than 5,000 texts. A half-yearly publication, PrimaPersona, produced by the Foundation is on sale in branches of the Feltrinelli bookshop throughout Italy.

The premises serve not as a museum but as a library. And, unless stated to the contrary, the texts are available for consultation by scholars and the general public alike. Furthermore, more than a hundred university degree theses have been dedicated to this phenomenon (and their number increases each year); these too are available for consultation. From a material point of view, one of the most original works in the Archives comprises the personal memoirs of Clelia Marchi: after the death of her husband in 1984, she began to write the story of her life on her bed sheets.

SIGHTS NEARBY:

THE CAMPARI FOUNTAIN

❷

Piazza Caduti
52010 Chiusi della Verna (AR)
This fountain advertising Campari was produced in 1931 by the sculptor Giuseppe Gronchi. It was the first of a series of twelve identical fountains created throughout Italy. Amongst those still extant is another at Le Piastre, outside Pistoia.

MUSEUM OF GUN POWDER AND SMUGGLING ❸

Via Verna
52010 Chitignano (AR)
• Opening hours: From the last Saturday in June to the first Sunday in September, 15.00-19.00. At other times, visits possible by appointment:
Tel: 0575 59 67 13 (8.00-14.00, except Sunday).
• Free admission.
• To walk to the "Gunpowder Factory of Hell": take the SP60 towards Verna. After a few bends in the road, the route is marked by a post bearing the number one, indicating the beginning of the footpath; there is not much car parking space. Now follow the footpath to the pillo [crushing plant].

A village that thrived on contraband

Set up in 2001, the Museum of Gunpowder and Smuggling in Chitignano is a fine way of paying homage to the village's disreputable past as a centre of contraband. In 1789 the Tuscan government forbade the sale of tobacco and introduced limits on how much could be grown for personal consumption. Threatened with the loss of one of their major sources of income, the inhabitants of Chitignano decided to ignore the ban and become smugglers, buying tobacco in Umbria, processing it in Chitignano, and then transporting it northwards.

Later, in 1830, the Grand Duchy of Tuscany introduced a total ban on the growing of tobacco. At this point, Chitignano looked for another source of income. There were already two licensed gunpowder factories in the area, so the inhabitants set to producing and distributing contraband gunpowder. The smugglers acquired the sulphur and saltpetre secretly and then produced charcoal using the wood of the area's abundant walnut trees.

The museum gives you a vivid picture of the activities of the smugglers. Furthermore, a ten-minute walk along a path marked by numbered posts brings you to the "Gunpowder Factory of Hell", which contains a fully func-

tional crushing plant built of wood. Driven by a waterwheel powered by a small stream flowing through this magnificent - and secluded - area of woodland, the plant was used to mix the three basic ingredients of gunpowder...

SIGHTS NEARBY:

MODEL IN THE MUSEUM OF THE BATTLE OF ANGHIARI

1-2, Piazza Mameli,. 52031 Anghiari (AR). Tel: 0575 78 70 23.

Opening hours: April to October, daily 9.00-19.00; November to March, Friday, Saturday and Sunday 9.00-13.00 and 15.00-19.00. Admission: 3.50 €.

A fine model recreates the Battle of Anghiari, which was of great importance in the history of Tuscany: fought on 29 June 1440, this clash between Florentine forces (commanded by Niccolò Piccinino) and a Milanese army resulted in a victory which saved Tuscany from becoming a dominion of the Duke of Milan. Machiavelli later gave this ironic account of the battle: "And if this combat which was so long that it lasted from twenty to twenty-four hours, not a single man died from wounds caused by weapons or other valorous feats of arms, but only as a result of falling from his horse and being trodden under hoof."

BALDACCIO'S GHOST STILL HAUNTS THE CASTELLO DI SORCI

Built during the 13th century, the Castello di Sorci [Castle of Mice] was for fifty years home to the family of Baldaccio d'Anghiari, a "soldier of fortune" (capitano di ventura) born around 1400. Baldaccio's career began when he recruited a band of mercenaries to pillage the surrounding area. He was twice sentenced to the gallows, but then "saved" by the Florentines whom he served on various occasions. Unfortunately for Baldaccio, he would denounce Bartolomeo Orlandini for cowardice in abandoning the castle of Marradi to the troops of another capitano di ventura (Niccolò Piccinino, 1386-1444; so-called because he was short of stature: piccinin). When Orlandini became Gonfaloniere di Giustizia* in Florence, he took revenge: on 6 September 1441, he summoned Baldaccio to Palazzo Vecchio, accused him of treason, had him stabbed several times and then hurled his body out of the window. Baldacci survived – only to be beheaded; afterwards his body was put on public display. Since that treacherous death, it would seem that Baldaccio's ghost has haunted his family castle, which can be visited by applying at the restaurant or (for group visits) by prior phone booking. Don't forget to try the wonderful home-made pasta, washed down with a good bottle of vino del fantasma.

"Castello di Sorci" Hotel . 52031 Anghiari (AR). Tel: 0575 78 90 66. E-mail: info@castellodisorci.it. www.castellodisorci.it

Closed Mondays. Visits to the castle : 1 €. Free for children. Vino del fantasma: 4 € per 3/4 litre. Directions: from Anghiari take the road to Arezzo, the castle stands about 3 km down the road.

* Gonfaloniere di Giustizia : the Gonfaloniere was originally the official entrusted with bearing the gonfalon, the town's standard. At the time of the Florentine Republic, the post was reserved to a member of the lower bourgeoisie, to serve as a counterweight to the power of the major dynasties within the town. Granted his own militia, he could impose his authority upon these aristocratic families. However, this balance of power did not last for long: by the 15th century, the gonfaloniere was being chosen from amongst the Medici or their allies.

CLOCK TOWER

❺

Castello di San Niccolò
52018 Castel San Niccolò (AR)
To find out more: www.nicolaseverino.it

The largest "Roman" clock face in Italy

The clock at the castle of San Niccolò is curious in that it has a "Roman" clock face – that is, one which marks out of the hours of the day from I to VI, rather than I to XII (see below). Whilst the castle itself dates back to the 13th century, the clock dates from 1806-1807 and its mechanism was replaced in 1863. It is of such massive size because it was intended to be visible to the peasants working in the surrounding fields.

THE MEASUREMENT OF TIME

The division of a day into hours probably began with the Chaldeans. We know that the Babylonians divided the day into 12 kaspars and the Chinese into 12 toki. The Greeks and the Romans would divide the day into two equal periods of twelve hours each. Given that the period of daylight varied according to the season, the length of these day or night hours could vary, with an hour of winter daytime being much shorter than an hour of winter night time.

The need for a more precise measurement of time was felt by certain rigorously disciplined monastic orders, particularly the Benedictines, who used sundials to fix the hours of prayers (matins, vespers, etc) with precision.

Mechanical clocks would make their first appearance in Europe at the end of the 13th century. This entailed a veritable revolution: now hours had a fixed length, and by the end of the 14th century, most cities had abandoned sundials and gnomons for mechanical clocks installed in church towers.

Beginning at sunset, the day was divided into 24 hours, with the clock face thus being marked from I to XXIV. However, it was soon realised that having to count up to 24 strokes of the clock in order to tell the time could lead to error.

In the 15th century a simplified system was adopted, with clocks striking a maximum of 6 times rather than 24. This simplification in counting the strokes of the hour was soon reflected in clock faces, which were now marked I to VI (like the one here at San Niccolò).

During the period of Napoleonic rule, this "Roman" clock face was replaced with the "French-style" clock face marked I to XII, with the day beginning not at sunset but at midnight.

HANNIBAL'S BRIDGE

Via di Annibale, Faltona. 52010 Talla (AR)
• Directions: leave your car in the small car park at the village of Faltona and then take the Via Annibale which starts at the entrance to the village. The path runs down to a gate (designed to keep animals in; remember to close it behind you). Continuing along the path, you come to a small stream (the Ginesso) and a new bridge. Cross over and a little further on you'll see the ruin of two bridges

Tradition has it that the Carthaginian general crossed by this Ponte d'Annibale in 217 BC during his long march to take on the forces of the Roman empire. The ruins of the two bridges would seem to date from the Middle Ages; however, it cannot be ruled out that they are built on Roman structures or occupy the site of a Roman bridge that no longer exists.

A bridge used by Hannibal and his elephants

Italy has other "Hannibal Bridges", generally mere crossing-points over streams or torrents where there is no longer any actual bridge. However, there are a number of extant Roman bridges which it is plausible to suppose were used by the Carthaginian army.

OTHER "HANNIBAL BRIDGES" IN ITALY

- The bridge of Gorgo Vecchio, at Cerreto Sannita, outside Benevento in Campania.
- The bridge of Rogliano, outside Cosenza in Calabria. This was demolished by the Romans to prevent Hannibal using it again, when he was fleeing northwards out of Italy.
- The bridge of Reggello outside Florence.
- The bridge of Guardialfiera, outside Campobasso (in Molise), in part submerged beneath the man-made lake of Guardialfiera.

HANNIBAL'S ROUTE OF INVASION
Third Century B.C.

Three other bridges are named after Hannibal, but it is unlikely he ever used them. They are at Rapallo (outside Genoa), Pinasca (outside Turin) and Incisa Val d'Arno (outside Florence).

The Route taken by Hannibal. The Department of History, United States Military Academy

KNOTTED COLUMNS IN THE CHURCH OF GROPINA ❷

Church of Saint-Pierre (Pieve di San Pietro)
Gropina
52024 Loro Ciuffenno (AR)
• Opening hours: In winter 8.00-12.00 and 15.00-17.00, summer, 8.00-12.00 and from 17.00-19.00.
• Directions: Take the Valdarno exit off the A1 motorway. Follow the SP1 to Loro Ciuffena. After driving through the town, continue on the same road (also called Via dei Sette Ponti) towards Arezzo. After 1.3 km, take the narrow unsurfaced road to the village of Gropina.

Why so many knots?

Built in the 12th century but incorporating structures that date back to the 4th and 8th century, the church in Gropina has a very austere interior – something which makes the imposing pulpit (part of the 8th century structure) all the more striking.

The pulpit itself rests on two knotted columns. The parish priest, Father Valente Moretti, explains their symbolism in these terms: "One of the columns

represents the Father, the other the Son, and the knot which unites them, the Holy Spirit. The whole ensemble forms the Holy Trinity." According to others, the symbol could refer to the two (human and divine) natures of the Son of God, bound together in a single person. There is also a knot within one of the columns on the outside of the apse, although in this case Father Moretti sees it solely as a decorative motif.

TROMPE-L'OEIL CUPOLA IN THE CHURCH OF LA BADIA

❽

Piazza della Badia
52100 Arezzo (AR)

A cupola that is an illusion

Built by Benedictine monks in the 13th century, the church of Sante Flora e Lucilla was altered extensively by Giorgio Vasari in 1565. It has an astonishing trompe-l'oeil cupola created by Andrea Pozzo in 1702; recent restoration has made the optical illusion even more stunning in effect.

Andrea Pozzo created two other trompe-l'oeil cupolas: one in the university church of Vienna, the other in the church of San Ignazio in Rome (see Secret Rome, by the same publisher).

AREZZO, WHERE "LIFE IS BEAUTIFUL"

Roberto Benigni's famous film La vita è bella was shot partly on location in Arezzo, a city very dear to the director's heart; he was born not far away – in the village of Manciano Misericordia, in 1952. The commercial success of the film having promoted the image of the city throughout the world, the local Tourist Board decided to create a very special "itinerary" comprising the sights associated with the motion picture. Large panels at the eight major locations illustrate the scenes shot there with photographs and the corresponding dialogue.

The pamphlet with a map of the itinerary can be obtained from the Agenzia per il Turisomo di Arezzo (116, Piazza Risorgimento) or the Centro Di Informazione E Accoglienza Turistica (Sala San Sebastiano – 1, Via Ricasoli)

SIGHTS NEARBY:

❾

STATUE OF ROBERTO BENIGNI

Parco della Creatività
52040 Manciano (AR)
- Tel: 0575 65 34 01
- E-mail: androggi@tin.it
- www.parcodellacreativita.com

The idea of Andrea Roggi and Alessandro Neri, this statue of Roberto Benigni stands in his native village of Manciano Misericordia (about twenty kilometres from Arezzo). Made of bronze and stone and standing 4.5 metres high, it was officially unveiled in 1999. The director is shown

in a rather curious pose: holding his right foot in his right hand, he is waving with his left. The statue had not been in place long before someone broke off the right leg and stole it; the work has since been restored thanks to the Town Council. Opposite the statue, Andrea Roggi and other sculptors display their work in a garden entitled Il Parco della Creatività (open from 9am to 7pm).

MUSEUM OF THE GORI & ZUCCHI COMPANY (UNO A ERRE) ❿

550, Via Fiorentina,
52100 Arezzo (AR)
• Visits – either free or guided tours – by appointment only.
• Tel: 0575 92 54 03.
• E-mail: museo.info@unoaerre.it

> *Saddam Hussein's silver sword*

Photograph courtesy of the Uno A Erre company

One of the world's leading creators of jewellery and costume jewellery, Uno A Erre has a museum within its premises in Arezzo. Along with a wide range of the pieces which the company has manufactured since its foundation in 1926, there are also tools and instruments and various original designs.

One of the showcases contains the steel jewellery that was created in response to the Oro alla Patria [Gold for the Fatherland] campaign (see below).

The most unusual piece in the museum, however, is a silver sword that was presented to the dictator Saddam Hussein in 1986. This was the model for the 150 gold swords encrusted with precious stones that Saddam was going to present as gifts to the various sheiks who had supported him in the war against Iran. In fact, 100 of these swords were delivered, but the wars in which Iraq was involved from 1990 onwards led to production being suspended.

GOLD FOR THE FATHERLAND

In response to the Fascist invasion of Ethiopia, the League of Nations (the first attempt at a United Nations) imposed economic sanctions on Italy.

The Italian government's response was to collect as much gold as possible from individual citizens, given that the currency of the day was still bound to the gold standard. 18 December thus became "Confidence Day", with married couples offering their gold wedding rings in exchange for rings of steel.

After 1940, the collection was extended to cover steel itself, required in armaments factories. Mussolini was not the first to come up with this idea: the governments of both France and Great Britain had launched similar campaigns during the First World War.

THE "DEAD MAN'S GATE" AT PALAZZO MANCINI ⑪

Via Dardano, 15
52044 Cortona (AR)

Showing the Grim Reaper the door...

To the left of the main doorway of Palazzo Mancini is a remarkable example of a "Dead Man's Gate". A frequent feature in medieval buildings, these doorways had one function: to give egress to coffins. The door was then shut immediately so that the dead had no chance of re-entering the building. The custom seems to have come from the Etruscans, who believed that death itself exited with the dead man and that it could only come back via the same doorway.

The subject is rather delicate, but it would seem that some of these doorways are still in use in Italy.

There is a second "Dead Man's Gate" in Cortona, at number 25 Via Roma; however, this one has been bricked in.

SIGHTS NEARBY:

SAINT GILIBERT'S WELL ⑫

Saint Gilibert is said to have transformed the water from this well into wine.
The local road to Manzano (recently renamed Viale Vannucio Faralli).
Monsigliolo. 52044 Cortona (AR)

The well is to the right of the local Manzano road which links Cortona with Foiano di Chiana. Just after the village of Monsigliolo there is a plaque which records a popular tradition that, in the year 515, St. Gilibert passed through here on a pilgrimage (probably heading for Rome) and stopped at this well, which is now named after him. To thank the peasant farmer for his hospitality, he changed the water drawn from the well into wine.

PONTE BURIANO
13

52100 Arezzo

Mona Lisa's bridge?

Built in 1277, the present Ponte Buriano would seem to stand on the site of a bridge built by the Etruscans to link the two cities of Arezzo and Fiesole. The span of that bridge rested on massive tree trunks, and the structure would later be incorporated by the Romans into their Via Cassia, which ran from Rome to Florence by way of Arezzo. The present bridge has survived thanks to the extraordinary efficiency of the bomb squads working with the Allied forces in 1944, who managed to defuse explosive charges set by the Germans as they retreated. We know that in 1502 Leonardo da Vinci was commissioned by Cesare Borgia to draw up a map of this part of Tuscany. These maps now known as the "Windsor Maps" because they form part of the Royal Collection at Windsor Castle – show the Ponte Buriano. This fact has led some to conclude, perhaps rather hastily, that the bridge in question is the same as that which appears in the background to the right of the Mona Lisa. The supporters of this theory point out that the landscape on the left of the sitter has two other features typical of the area around Arezzo: meandering waterways entering a gorge, and marlaceous terrain. Others have argued that Leonardo simply created an imaginary landscape made up of elements taken from various places. It should be noted, however, that no other bridge has been put forward as a possible source for that which appears in the great painting.

SIGHTS NEARBY:

IVAN BRUSCHI'S HOME MUSEUM
14

14, Corso Italia. 52100 Arezzo (AR)
- Tel: 0575 35 41 26 • E-mail: info@fondazionebruschi.it
- www.fondazionebruschi.it
- Opening hours: Tuesday to Sunday 10.00-13.00 and 17.00-19.00 (winter: 14.00-18.00).
- Admission: 3 €, reduced: 2 €.

A visit to this home-museum gives you an insight into the world of a 20th century visionary. An antiquarian and collector, Ivan Bruschi had a love of all things beautiful, and his magnificent home bears witness to a life dedicated to discovering the rare and notable artefacts of the past. What makes the place so unusual are the objects and furnishings that give us a very personal idea of this searcher after the curious and the intriguing. For example, the collection of coins (more than 4,000 extremely rare pieces) is housed in a piece of 18th century furniture. Composed of separate compartments which themselves contain a number of individual drawers, this piece of furniture is itself a little masterpiece of cabinet-making. Ivan Bruschi was also the original force behind the monthly Antiques Fair held in Arezzo, launching the very first one in 1968. The Fair is now held on the last Saturday/first Sunday of the month, from 8am to 8pm.

ELICIT ET
COLLIGIT

AD TVTIORA
EXPOSITORVM
CVNABVLA·1620

A · D ·   RECTORE
BVRGHESIO   DE SAMVELLI

CHARITATIS VBERA ET MELIORA VINO

MILK TAP AT THE OLD HOSPITAL OF THE FRATERNITÀ DI SANTA MARIA

⓯

Piazza XX Settembre
53043 Chiusi (SI)

> *An automatic milk dispenser, dating from the 17th century*

Against the wall inside the portico of the old hospital is the case which used to contain the "wheel" by means of which parents could leave their abandoned infants. The system worked on the same principle as that at the Ospedale degli Innocenti in Florence (see page 47).

Above this is a sort of twin-tube public dispenser in the form of two breasts. These would, upon demand, supply the children of poor families with milk. Two Latin inscriptions explain the purpose of this unusual facility, installed in 1620 thanks to a certain Borghese Samuelli. One reads Ad tutoria expositorum cunabula – 1620 and might be translated "For a safer sradle for foundlings". The second reads Charitatis ubera et meliora vino: the milk of charity is better than wine !

SIGHTS NEARBY:

TWO RIVAL TOWERS WITH ASTONISHING NAMES
⓰

At the Chiusi turn-off, the Villastrada road is flanked by two towers with astonishing names. One is Torre Beccati Questo [Take This Tower] and the other Torre Beccati Quello [Take That Tower]. In very different styles and some few hundred metres apart, one stands in Umbria and the other in Tuscany. They are clearly yet another expression of the ancient rivalry between the two regions.

STATUE OF TOTO IN THE CHURCH OF SAN BIAGIO
⓱

Church of San Biagio. Via di San Biagio. 53045 Montepulciano (SI)
To visit the sacristy: apply to the priest after services (mass times are displayed on the door).

Built outside the town walls of Montepulciano, San Biago is a splendid church designed by Antonio Sangallo the Elder. Two wooden statues in the sacristy depict the labourer Toto and his wife. A Latin plaque, dated 1659, records that Toto the peasant is being honoured for the energy he had put into raising funds for the building of the church. The plaque under the statue of his wife casts Toto in a rather less flattering light. It says that, suspecting his pregnant spouse of bearing the fruit of infidelity, he slit open her belly with a knife, only to reveal a foetus which, according to legend, addressed him with these words: "Sum tuus, parce ô pater !" [I am yours. Have pity, father!]

LPHABETICAL INDEX

THEMATIC INDEX

ARCHITECTURE

ARTS AND LITERATURE

THEMATIC INDEX

THEMATIC INDEX

CHILDREN

HISTORY AND PRE-HISTORY

THEMATIC INDEX

RELIGION AND ESOTERICA

THEMATIC INDEX